Collins
COBUILD

Key Words for
Hospitality

HarperCollins Publishers
Westerhill Road
Bishopbriggs
Glasgow
G64 2QT

First Edition 2013

Reprint 10 9 8 7 6 5 4 3 2 1 0

© HarperCollins Publishers 2013

ISBN 978-0-00-748981-7

Collins® and COBUILD® are
registered trademarks of
HarperCollins Publishers Limited

www.collinslanguage.com

A catalogue record for this book is
available from the British Library

CD recorded by Networks SRL,
Milan, Italy

Typeset by Davidson Publishing
Solutions, Glasgow

Printed in Great Britain by Clays Ltd,
St Ives plc

Acknowledgements

We would like to thank those authors
and publishers who kindly gave
permission for copyright material
to be used in the Collins Corpus.
We would also like to thank Times
Newspapers Ltd for providing
valuable data.

Contents

Contributors

Specialist consultant
Mike Seymour, author of *Hotel and Hospitality English*
and *English for Insurance Professionals*, and contributor
to German EFL magazine *Business Spotlight*

Project manager
Patrick White

Editors
Katherine Carroll
Mary O'Neill
Enid Pearsons
Elizabeth Walter
Kate Woodford

Computing support
Mark Taylor

For the publisher
Gerry Breslin
Lucy Cooper
Kerry Ferguson
Gavin Gray
Elaine Higgleton
Persephone Lock
Ruth O'Donovan
Rosie Pearce
Lisa Sutherland

Introduction

Collins COBUILD Key Words for Hospitality is a brand-new vocabulary book for students who want to master the English of Hospitality in order to study or work in the field. This title contains the 500 most important English words and phrases relating to Hospitality, as well as a range of additional features which have been specially designed to help you to *really* understand and use the language of this specific area.

The main body of the book contains alphabetically organized dictionary-style entries for the key words and phrases of Hospitality. These vocabulary items have been specially chosen to fully prepare you for the type of language that you will need in this field. Many are specialized terms that are very specific to this profession and area of study. Others are more common or general words and phrases that are often used in the context of Hospitality.

Each word and phrase is explained clearly and precisely, in English that is easy to understand. In addition, each entry is illustrated with examples taken from the Collins Corpus. Of course, you will also find grammatical information about the way that the words and phrases behave.

In amongst the alphabetically organized entries, you will find valuable word-building features that will help you gain a better understanding of this area of English. For example, some features provide extra help with tricky pronunciations, while others pull together groups of related words that can usefully be learned as a set.

At the start of this book you will see lists of words and phrases, helpfully organized by topic area. You can use these lists to revise sets of vocabulary and to prepare for writing tasks. You will also find with this book an MP3 CD, containing a recording of each headword in the book, followed by an example sentence. This will help you to learn and remember pronunciations of words and phrases. Furthermore, the exercise section at the end of this book gives you an opportunity to memorize important words and phrases, to assess what you have learned, and to work out which areas still need attention.

So whether you are studying Hospitality, or you are already working in the field and intend to improve your career prospects, we are confident that *Collins COBUILD Key Words for Hospitality* will equip you for success in the future.

Guide to Dictionary Entries

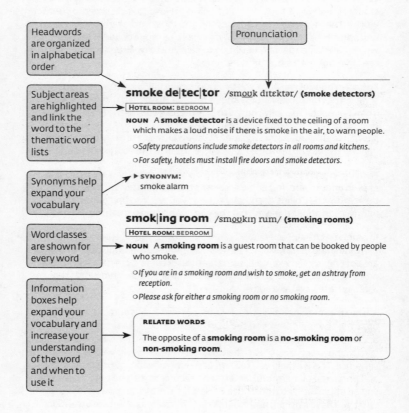

Headwords are organized in alphabetical order

Pronunciation

Subject areas are highlighted and link the word to the thematic word lists

smoke de|tec|tor /smoʊk dɪtɛktər/ **(smoke detectors)**

HOTEL ROOM: BEDROOM

NOUN A **smoke detector** is a device fixed to the ceiling of a room which makes a loud noise if there is smoke in the air, to warn people.

○ *Safety precautions include smoke detectors in all rooms and kitchens.*

○ *For safety, hotels must install fire doors and smoke detectors.*

Synonyms help expand your vocabulary

▶ **SYNONYM:**
smoke alarm

smok|ing room /smoʊkɪŋ rum/ **(smoking rooms)**

HOTEL ROOM: BEDROOM

Word classes are shown for every word

NOUN A **smoking room** is a guest room that can be booked by people who smoke.

○ *If you are in a smoking room and wish to smoke, get an ashtray from reception.*

○ *Please ask for either a smoking room or no smoking room.*

Information boxes help expand your vocabulary and increase your understanding of the word and when to use it

RELATED WORDS

The opposite of a **smoking room** is a **no-smoking room** or **non-smoking room**.

Guide to Dictionary Entries

All the different forms of the word are listed

a|pol|o|gize /əpɒlədʒaɪz/ **(apologizes, apologized, apologizing)**

GENERAL

Definitions explain what the word means in simple language

VERB When you **apologize** to someone, you say that you are sorry that you have caused trouble for them.

○ *The guest apologized for arriving late.*

○ *The manager apologized to the people who had been affected by the leak.*

Examples show how the word is used in context

▶ **COLLOCATIONS:**
apologize for
apologize to

Collocations help you put the word into practice

room oc|cu|pan|cy tax (ABBR **ROT**) /rum ɒkyəpənsi tæks/

GENERAL

NOUN **Room occupancy tax** is a tax that guests at a hotel have to pay in order to stay there.

○ *The 6 percent room occupancy tax applies to any room in the hotel.*

○ *There is a 14% sales tax plus a $2 per night room occupancy tax.*

Variants of the headword, such as abbreviated, full forms and British forms, are also shown

Guide to Pronunciation Symbols

Vowel Sounds

ɑ	calm, ah
ɑr	heart, far
æ	act, mass
ɑɪ	dive, cry
ɑɪər	fire, tire
ɑʊ	out, down
ɑʊər	flour, sour
ɛ	met, lend, pen
eɪ	say, weight
ɛər	fair, care
ɪ	fit, win
i	feed, me
ɪər	near, beard
ɒ	lot, spot
oʊ	note, coat
ɔ	claw, bought
ɔr	more, cord
ɔɪ	boy, joint
ʊ	could, stood
u	you, use
ʊər	lure, endure
ɜr	turn, third
ʌ	fund, must
ə	*the first vowel in* **a**bout
ər	*the first vowel in* **fo**rgotten
i	*the second vowel in* ver**y**
u	*the second vowel in* act**u**al

Consonant Sounds

b	bed, rub
d	done, red
f	fit, if
g	good, dog
h	hat, horse
y	yellow, you
k	king, pick
l	lip, bill
ᵊl	handle, panel
m	mat, ram
n	not, tin
ᵊn	hidden, written
p	pay, lip
r	run, read
s	soon, bus
t	talk, bet
v	van, love
w	win, wool
ʍ	why, wheat
z	zoo, buzz
ʃ	ship, wish
ʒ	measure, leisure
ŋ	sing, working
tʃ	cheap, witch
θ	thin, myth
ð	then, other
dʒ	joy, bridge

Word Lists

FOOD AND DRINK
alcoholic drinks
beer
bottled beer
brandy
champagne
cognac
dessert wine
dry white wine
dry wine
liquor
medium dry white wine
red wine
vintage

breakfast
boiled egg
bread
butter
cereals
coffee
continental breakfast
croissant
Danish pastry
decaffeinated coffee
eggs
English breakfast
freshly squeezed
fried egg
fruit juice
granola
hash browns
jelly
milk
omelet
over easy
pancake
roll
room key
sausage
scrambled eggs
sugar
sunny side up
sweetener
teapot
toast

cooking
barbecue
boil
boiled
carve
cook
deep-fried
freeze
fried
frozen
fry
medium well
pour
serve
taste
warm

dining
à la carte
aperitif
appetizer
ask for the check
bread basket
clear a table
complain about the food
confirm a reservation
dessert
entrée
fixed-price menu
four-course meal
ice cream
ice cube
order
pay
prix fixe
pudding
see the menu

set menu
sewing kit
shaving mirror
tip

fish and seafood
calamari
clam
langoustine
lobster
mussels
oyster
prawn
salmon
seafood
shellfish
sushi

fruit
banana
cherry
grape
grapefruit
kiwi fruit
lemon
lime
melon
orange

herbs and spices
black pepper
salt
sea salt

meat
bacon
beef
casserole
chicken
chop
cold cuts
cold meat

duck
escalope
fillet
game
goose
ham
lamb
medium
medium rare
pâté
pork
poultry
rare
salami
sauce
steak
well done

vegetables
cabbage
carrot
cauliflower
celery
coleslaw
French fries
fried potato
garlic
gherkin
lettuce
olive
onion
potato
tomato

GENERAL
apologize
apology
brochure
event
function
function room
housekeeping

leave feedback
lend
liability
lobby
make a complaint
order room service
reception
repair
reservations manager
restaurant
revolving door
room occupancy tax
room service
service a room
valuables

HOTEL BAR

bar
bar stool
bartender
beer glass
beverage
bottle top
cocktail
cocktail shaker
cork
corkscrew
happy hour
hard-boiled egg
head waiter
health club
ice
measure
meeting room
meetings and conference manager
mineral water
mix a drink
mixer
on tap
open a bottle
order a drink
root beer

rosé wine
shot
shot glass
soda water
sparkling mineral water
sparkling wine
tea
white wine

HOTEL EQUIPMENT

fire extinguisher
first sitting
fish course
fitness center
key card

HOTEL FACILITIES

amenities
baggage storage room
ballroom
banquet room
business center
conference facilities
conference room
corridor
elevator
evacuation route
facilities
fire door
fire escape
florist
guest services
gym
hairdresser
hall
host an event
in-suite dining
Internet access
laundry service
movies on demand
parking garage
parking lot

safe deposit box
sales manager
spa
spa and wellness facilities
spare ribs
spirits
store baggage
swimming pool
valet parking

business center
fax
make a photocopy
photocopier
photocopy
printer
priority check-in
priority guest
queen-sized bed
rack rate
send a fax

HOTEL PERSONNEL
assistant manager
bellhop
bellman
chambermaid
concierge
doorman
duty manager
food and beverage manager
front of house manager
general manager
housekeeper
housekeeping cart
maid
maitre d'
porter
receptionist
second sitting
security guard
uniform

HOTEL ROOM
accessible room
sugar cube
suite
superior room
wake-up call
wall socket
wastebasket

bathroom
bathmat
bathrobe
bath towel
bathtub
drain
faucet
glass
grab handle
hand towel
hotel limo
hotel limo driver
hot tub
Jacuzzi
mirror
plug
poached egg
razor
shampoo
shower
soap
toothbrush
toothpaste
towel
turn-down service

bedroom
air conditioning
alarm clock
bed
bedding
blanket
bunk beds

carpet
channel
closet
comforter
cushion
docking station
do not disturb sign
door chain
door handle
double bed
double measure
double room
drapes
drawers
duvet
duvet cover
early check-in
feather pillow
feedback form
flat-screen television
hairdryer
hanger
ice bucket
ice machine
king-sized bed
lock
low floor
mattress
minibar
notice
outlet
pants press
pay TV
pillow
pillowcase
please clean my room sign
radio
remote control
rug
safe
sheet
single room

slippers
smoke detector
smoking room
snacks
soft-boiled egg
soft drinks
sommelier
soup bowl
telephone
twin bed
voice mail
wardrobe
wireless Internet

breakfast
television
three-course meal

HOUSEKEEPING AND MAINTENANCE

change the sheets
clean a room
cloth
dust
duster
empty the wastebasket
fix
furniture polish
inspect
make the bed
polish
replace
replenish
restock
sweep
tidy
vacuum
vacuum cleaner

RESERVATIONS AND CHECKING IN AND OUT

accept a card
accommodations
add to the check
advance purchase booking
all meals included
arrival date
ask for a signature
ask for feedback
bed and breakfast
breakfast and dinner
cancel a reservation
cancellation deadline
cancellation fee
change a reservation
check in
check-in time
check out
check-out time
comp
complaint
corporate rate
coupon
credit card guarantee
daily newspaper
deduct from the bill
departure date
deposit
discount
expiration date
fully booked
hold a reservation
incidental charges
included
late check-out
laundry bag
line
mezzanine
modify a reservation
no vacancies
package

refuse a card
reservation
reserve a room
respond to a complaint
reverse a charge
room only
sales tax
tariff
upgrade
upper floor
vacancy
voucher
wait in a line
walk-up rate

RESTAURANT

buffet line
hors d'oeuvres
show to a table
side dish
wine list

dining

party

equipment

bread plate
butter knife
chair
champagne bucket
cup
dessert bowl
dessert menu
dessert spoon
digestif
dinner plate
fish knife
flatware
fork
knife
menu
napkin

nonalcoholic beer
no-smoking room
no smoking sign
occupancy rate
pitcher
plate
silverware
soup spoon
spoon
table
tablecloth
tableware
tray
wine bucket
wine cooler
wine glass

paying the check

bring the check
charge to a room
check
cover charge
credit card terminal

crib
discretionary service charge
gratuity
guest relations manager
guest services manager
optional
pay the check
print
receipt
round up
service charge
sign a check
signature

personnel

bus boy
busser
chef
host
hostess
waiter
waitperson
waitress

A–Z

Aa

---

ac|cept a card /æksɛpt ə kɑrd/ (accepts a card, accepted a card, accepting a card)

PHRASE If a hotel or restaurant **accepts a card**, they agree that a credit card can be used to pay the bill.

- ○ Do not accept a card after the expiration date.
- ○ Most large hotels accept major credit cards as payment.

---

ac|ces|si|ble room /æksɛsɪbᵊl rum/ (accessible rooms)

NOUN An **accessible room** is a room that is easy for disabled people to enter and leave.

- ○ The accessible room is on the first floor.
- ○ The accessible rooms have wider doorways to the bedroom and bathroom.

---

ac|com|mo|da|tions /əkɒmədeɪʃənz/

NOUN **Accommodations** are hotels or rooms where people can stay for a period of time.

- ○ Some of the guests were not satisfied with their accommodations.
- ○ The resort offers a wide choice of accommodations, from single rooms to suites.

A

US/UK ENGLISH

Note that British speakers of English usually use the singular form, **accommodation**.

○ *Have you booked your accommodation yet?*

---

add to the check (in BRIT use **bill**) /æd tə ðə tʃɛk/ (**adds to the check, added to the check, adding to the check**)

RESERVATIONS AND CHECKING IN AND OUT

PHRASE If you **add** an item or expense **to the check** at a restaurant or hotel, you put an extra charge onto a customer's bill to charge for an additional service they have used.

○ *Any room service charges are added to your check.*

○ *The menu price of each item ordered will be added to the check at the end of the meal.*

---

ad|vance pur|chase book|ing /ædvæns pɜrtʃɪs bʊkɪŋ/ (**advance purchase bookings**)

RESERVATIONS AND CHECKING IN AND OUT

COUNT/NONCOUNT NOUN **Advance purchase booking** is an arrangement that allows you to book and pay for a hotel room before you arrive, usually at a discounted rate.

○ *Discounts are available on advance purchase booking.*

○ *You can now make an advance purchase booking for the hotel a month before your stay.*

---

air con|di|tion|ing /ɛər kəndɪʃənɪŋ/

HOTEL ROOM: BEDROOM

NOUN **Air conditioning** is a method of providing buildings and vehicles with cool dry air.

○ *All rooms have TV, telephone, and air conditioning.*

○ *The room is too hot. Is the air conditioning working?*

à la carte¹ /ɑ lə kɑrt/

FOOD AND DRINK: DINING

ADJECTIVE An **à la carte** menu in a restaurant offers you a choice of individually priced dishes for each course.

○ You can choose as much or as little as you want from the à la carte menu.

○ The set menu is $20; a three-course à la carte dinner costs around $37.

▶ **COLLOCATION:**
à la carte menu

RELATED WORDS

Compare **à la carte** with **set menu** or **prix fixe**, which is a menu with a specific set of meals to choose from where the price charged for each meal is the same.

WORD ORIGINS

Note that **à la carte** is a French phrase, meaning "according to the menu."

à la carte² /ɑ lə kɑrt/

FOOD AND DRINK: DINING

ADVERB If you eat **à la carte**, you order food from an à la carte menu.

○ A set meal is 35 dollars, or you can eat à la carte.

○ Eating à la carte is much more expensive than choosing the set menu.

▶ **COLLOCATIONS:**
dine à la carte
eat à la carte

a|larm clock /əlɑrm klɒk/ (alarm clocks)

HOTEL ROOM: BEDROOM

NOUN An **alarm clock** is a clock that you can set to make a noise so that it wakes you up at a particular time.

A

○ *Is there an alarm clock in the room?*

○ *The alarm clock doesn't work and I overslept.*

WORDS USED WITH "ALARM CLOCK"

If you **set** an alarm clock, you press buttons on it so that it will make a noise at a particular time, and if an alarm clock **goes off**, it starts to make a noise.

---

all meals in|clud|ed (in BRIT use **full board**) /ɔl miːlz ɪnkluːdɪd/

RESERVATIONS AND CHECKING IN AND OUT

PHRASE **All meals included** is used to indicate that a price, especially the price of a hotel stay or vacation, includes the cost of meals in the hotel.

○ *Stay overnight in a suite at the hotel, all meals included.*

○ *There is 50% off accommodation, with all meals included in the price.*

RELATED WORDS

The following terms indicate which meals are included when you pay a particular price to stay at a hotel:

bed and breakfast
an arrangement by which you pay for a room for the night and for breakfast the following morning

breakfast and dinner
an arrangement by which you pay for a room for the night and for breakfast and dinner the following day

room only
used to indicate that the price does not include the cost of food

---

a|men|i|ties /əmɛnɪtiz/

HOTEL FACILITIES

NOUN **Amenities** are things such as stores or sports facilities that are provided for people's convenience, enjoyment, or comfort.

○ The hotel amenities include health clubs, conference facilities, and banqueting rooms.

○ The city has tried to update its tourist amenities by building new hotels and information centers.

---

a|pe|ri|tif /æpɛrɪtiːf/ (aperitifs)

FOOD AND DRINK: DINING

NOUN An **aperitif** is an alcoholic drink that you have before a meal.

○ Would you like an aperitif before dinner?

○ Dinner is $40 per person and includes an aperitif before dinner.

---

a|pol|o|gize /əpɒlədʒaɪz/ (apologizes, apologized, apologizing)

GENERAL

VERB When you **apologize** to someone, you say that you are sorry that you have caused trouble for them.

○ The guest apologized for arriving late.

○ The manager apologized to the people who had been affected by the leak.

▶ COLLOCATIONS:
apologize for
apologize to

USEFUL PHRASES
Apologizing formally

The simplest way of apologizing for something that is not serious is to say **I'm sorry** or (for more emphasis), **I'm very sorry** or **I'm so sorry**.

○ I'm sorry, Ma'am, I didn't hear what you said.

○ My colleague has misspelled your name – I'm so sorry.

More formal ways of apologizing are **I do apologize** and **I beg your pardon**.

○ I do apologize for mispronouncing your name just now.

○ I understand the table was booked for the wrong time, Sir. I beg your pardon.

A

> To make a very formal apology, especially in writing, use **Please accept my/our apologies**.
>
> ○ Please accept our apologies for any inconvenience caused.

---

a|pol|o|gy /əpɒlədʒi/ (apologies)

GENERAL

NOUN An **apology** is something that you say or write in order to tell someone you are sorry that you have caused trouble for them.

○ I didn't get an apology for the mistake.

○ He wrote a letter of complaint to the manager and received a letter of apology.

▶ COLLOCATION:
make an apology

> **TALKING ABOUT APOLOGIES**
>
> To **make** an apology is to say sorry for something you have done, especially in a formal context.
>
> You might say you **owe** someone an apology if you feel you must say sorry to them for something you have done.
>
> To **accept** someone's apology is to say that you understand that someone is sorry and are no longer angry with them.
>
> To **demand** an apology is to tell someone that they must say sorry for something they have done.

---

ap|pe|tiz|er (in BRIT use starter) /æpɪtaɪzər/ (appetizers)

FOOD AND DRINK: DINING

NOUN An **appetizer** is the first course of a meal. It consists of a small amount of food.

○ Dinner will include an appetizer with an entrée and dessert.

○ He ordered the pasta appetizer then the chicken entrée.

> **RELATED WORDS**
>
> Compare **appetizer** with **entrée**, which is the main course, or sometimes a dish before the main course, and **dessert**, which is the sweet food that you eat at the end of a meal.

---

ar|ri|val date /əraɪvªl deɪt/ (**arrival dates**)

RESERVATIONS AND CHECKING IN AND OUT

NOUN Your **arrival date** is the date that you are expected to come to a hotel or other location.

○ *If you need to cancel your reservation, you must notify us at least five days prior to your scheduled arrival date.*

○ *His exact arrival date is not known so we cannot reserve a room.*

> **RELATED WORDS**
>
> Compare **arrival date** with **departure date**, which is the date that you are expected to leave a hotel or other location.

---

ask for a sig|na|ture /æsk fər ə sɪgnətʃər/ (**asks for a signature, asked for a signature, asking for a signature**)

RESERVATIONS AND CHECKING IN AND OUT

PHRASE If you **ask for a signature**, you ask someone to write their name, in their own characteristic way, on a document.

○ *At check-in, the assistant checks your ID and asks you for a signature.*

○ *Staff need to ask for your signature in order to prove that the card you are using is your own.*

---

ask for feed|back /æsk fər fidbæk/ (**asks for feedback, asked for feedback, asking for feedback**)

RESERVATIONS AND CHECKING IN AND OUT

PHRASE If you **ask for feedback**, you ask someone, such as a guest in a hotel, to tell you if they enjoyed their stay and what could be improved.

A

○ They review how good their service is by asking for feedback from customers.

○ The new manager asked for feedback from staff about possible improvements.

---

ask for the check (in BRIT use **ask for the bill**) /æsk fər ðə tʃɛk/ (**asks for the check, asked for the check, asking for the check**)

FOOD AND DRINK: DINING

PHRASE If you **ask for the check**, you ask the waitperson in a restaurant to bring you a piece of paper on which the price of your meal is written.

○ After coffee, he asked for the check.

○ They asked for the check, paid, and left the restaurant.

---

as|sis|tant man|ag|er /əsɪstənt mænɪdʒər/ (**assistant managers**)

HOTEL PERSONNEL

NOUN An **assistant manager** is one rank lower than a manager in a hotel, restaurant, or other workplace. Their job is to help the manager in their work.

○ She was working at the hotel as an assistant manager.

○ They are interviewing candidates for an assistant manager to help the manager.

HOTEL MANAGEMENT ROLES

The following are other management roles in a hotel:

duty manager, food and beverage manager, front of house manager, general manager, guest relations manager, guest services manager, meetings and conference manager, reservations manager, sales manager

Bb

---

ba|con /beɪkən/

FOOD AND DRINK: MEAT

NOUN **Bacon** is salted or smoked meat which comes from the back or sides of a pig.

○ *Breakfast comprises two eggs, two pieces of bacon, toast, and fresh fruit.*

○ *I didn't order the bacon and eggs for breakfast.*

▶ **COLLOCATIONS:**
fried bacon
smoked bacon

---

bag|gage stor|age room /bægɪdʒ stɔrɪdʒ rum/
(baggage storage rooms)

HOTEL FACILITIES

NOUN A **baggage storage room** is a room in a hotel where people can leave their baggage in order to collect it later.

○ *A baggage storage room is available for guests who want to leave bags.*

○ *The baggage storage room was too small to hold many bags.*

▶ **SYNONYM:**
luggage storage room

---

ball|room /bɔlrum/ (**ballrooms**)

HOTEL FACILITIES

NOUN A **ballroom** is a very large room that is used for dancing.

○ *Our ballroom is available for dances and concerts.*

○ *Our ballroom accommodates over 300 guests and has a large dance floor.*

B

ba|na|na /bənænə/ (bananas)

FOOD AND DRINK: FRUIT

NOUN **Bananas** are long curved fruit with yellow skins.

○ The plate of fruit contains a bunch of bananas, grapefruit, and oranges.

○ The bananas have turned from yellow to brown.

---

ban|quet room /bæŋkwɪt rum/ (banquet rooms)

HOTEL FACILITIES

NOUN A **banquet room** is a room in a hotel where large formal meals for many people can be held.

○ At special events, guests have a four-course meal in the banquet room.

○ A meeting was arranged in the hotel banquet room.

▶ **SYNONYM:**
banquet hall

---

bar¹ /bɑɪ/ (bars)

HOTEL BAR

NOUN A **bar** is a room in a hotel or other establishment where alcoholic drinks are served.

○ The hotel bar is open from 7pm until 10:30pm, with happy hour from 7pm to 8pm.

○ There's a nice bar across the street that serves excellent wines.

---

bar² /bɑɪ/ (bars)

HOTEL BAR

NOUN A **bar** is a counter on which alcoholic drinks are served.

○ Several guests were drinking at the bar.

○ The customer stood by the bar while the bartender brought his drink.

b

bar|be|cue /bɑrbɪkyu/ (barbecues, barbecued, barbecuing)

FOOD AND DRINK: COOKING

VERB If you **barbecue** food, especially meat, you cook it on a grill, usually over charcoal and with a highly flavored sauce.

○ *Tuna can be grilled, fried, or barbecued.*

○ *After we cover the burgers in sauce, we barbecue them on a hot grill for ten minutes.*

bar stool /bɑr stul/ (bar stools)

HOTEL BAR

NOUN A **bar stool** is a high chair with no back that you sit on at a bar.

○ *There is room in the bar for two tables and ten bar stools.*

○ *He sat on the high bar stool and ordered a drink.*

bar|tend|er /bɑrtɛndər/ (bartenders)

HOTEL BAR

NOUN A **bartender** is a person who serves drinks behind a bar.

○ *The bartender fetched the empty glasses.*

○ *I worked as a bartender behind the bar of a hotel.*

▶ **SYNONYMS:**
barkeeper
barmaid
barman

bath|mat /bæθmæt/ (bathmats)

HOTEL ROOM: BATHROOM

NOUN A **bathmat** is a mat that you stand on while you dry yourself after getting out of the bathtub or shower.

○ *There is a bathmat as well as two towels in the bathroom.*

○ *Replace the bathmat beside the shower if it is wet or badly soiled.*

bath|robe (ABBR robe) /bæθroʊb/ (bathrobes)

HOTEL ROOM: BATHROOM

NOUN A **bathrobe** is a loose piece of clothing usually made of the same material as towels. You wear it before or after you take a bath or a shower.

○ The suite has slippers and bathrobes for use during your stay.

○ All bathrooms have toweling bathrobes and well-stocked cabinets.

bath tow|el /bæθ taʊəl/ (bath towels)

HOTEL ROOM: BATHROOM

NOUN A **bath towel** is a large towel used for drying your body after you have taken a bath or shower.

○ Place your bath towels in the bathtub if you would like fresh ones.

○ The hand towels and bath towels in the bathroom look clean.

bath|tub /bæθtʌb/ (bathtubs)

HOTEL ROOM: BATHROOM

NOUN A **bathtub** is a long, usually rectangular container that you fill with water and sit in to wash your body.

○ The bathroom has a huge pink marble bathtub.

○ Does the bathroom have a bathtub or a shower?

bed /bɛd/ (beds)

HOTEL ROOM: BEDROOM

NOUN A **bed** is a piece of furniture that you lie on when you sleep.

○ The accommodation has up to 150 beds.

○ Most guests are ready to go to bed by 11 p.m.

BED VOCABULARY

The following are terms for items relating to beds:

bedding, blanket, comforter, duvet, duvet cover, feather pillow, mattress, pillow, pillowcase, sheet

bed and break|fast¹ (ABBR **B&B**) /bɛd ən brɛkfəst/ (**bed and breakfasts**)

RESERVATIONS AND CHECKING IN AND OUT

NOUN A **bed and breakfast** is a guest house that provides bed and breakfast accommodations. The abbreviation **B&B** is also used.

○ Enjoy discounts at hundreds of bed and breakfasts around the country.

○ The couple opened a bed and breakfast in an old farmhouse.

bed and break|fast² (ABBR **B&B**) /bɛd ən brɛkfəst/

RESERVATIONS AND CHECKING IN AND OUT

NOUN **Bed and breakfast** is a system of accommodations in a hotel or guest house, in which you pay for a room for the night and for breakfast the following morning. The abbreviation **B&B** is also used.

○ Bed and breakfast costs from $50 per person per night.

○ They will charge less for bed and breakfast than for dinner, bed and breakfast.

bed|ding /bɛdɪŋ/

HOTEL ROOM: BEDROOM

NOUN **Bedding** is sheets, blankets, and covers that are used on beds.

○ The bedding is changed every day.

○ To keep a bed clean, regularly wash the bedding.

▶ **SYNONYM:**
bed linen

beef /bif/

FOOD AND DRINK: MEAT

NOUN **Beef** is the meat of a cow, bull, or ox.

○ Our beef all comes from locally bred cows.

○ The burgers are made with 100 percent beef.

B

beer /bɪər/ (beers)

FOOD AND DRINK: ALCOHOLIC DRINKS

COUNT/NONCOUNT NOUN **Beer** is an alcoholic drink made from grain, served in a glass, can, or bottle.

○ *The man ordered a pint of beer.*

○ *The hotel opened a bar serving beer and wine a few years ago.*

▶ **COLLOCATIONS:**
glass of beer
pint of beer

beer glass /bɪər glæs/ (beer glasses)

HOTEL BAR

NOUN A **beer glass** is a glass, usually with no stem, which you use for drinking beer.

○ *Please return your empty beer glass to the bar.*

○ *You can fill beer glasses to the top.*

bell‖hop /bɛlhɒp/ (bellhops)

HOTEL PERSONNEL

NOUN A **bellhop** is a man or boy who works in a hotel, carrying bags or bringing things to the guests' rooms.

○ *Our bellhop will take your bags to your room.*

○ *The bellhop will open the door for you and carry your baggage.*

▶ **SYNONYM:**
bellboy

bell‖man /bɛlmən/ (bellmen)

HOTEL PERSONNEL

NOUN A **bellman** is a man who works in a hotel, carrying bags or bringing things to the guests' rooms.

○ *He loaded boxes and suitcases onto a bellman's cart.*

○ *He works as a bellman at the hotel, carrying guests' baggage.*

bev|er|age /bɛvərɪdʒ/ (beverages)

HOTEL BAR

NOUN **Beverages** are drinks. A less formal word is drink.

○ *Beverages are served in the hotel lounge.*

○ *Would you like a cold beverage with your snack?*

black pep|per /blæk pɛpər/

FOOD AND DRINK: HERBS AND SPICES

NOUN **Black pepper** is pepper which is dark in color and has been made from the dried berries of the pepper plant.

○ *Do you want black pepper on your soup?*

○ *If I don't have any white pepper can I use black pepper?*

blan|ket /blæŋkɪt/ (blankets)

HOTEL ROOM: BEDROOM

NOUN A **blanket** is a large square or rectangular piece of thick cloth, especially one that you put on a bed to keep you warm.

○ *Extra blankets and soft pillows are provided for your comfort.*

○ *If you are cold, you can ask for an extra blanket on your bed.*

boil¹ /bɔɪl/ (boils, boiled, boiling)

FOOD AND DRINK: COOKING

TRANSITIVE/INTRANSITIVE VERB When a hot liquid **boils** or when you **boil** it, bubbles appear in it and it starts to change into steam or vapor.

○ *Boil the water in the saucepan and add the butter.*

○ *I waited for the water to boil before I put the potatoes into the pot.*

▶ **COLLOCATION:**
  boil water

B

boil² /bɔɪl/ (boils, boiled, boiling)

FOOD AND DRINK: COOKING

TRANSITIVE/INTRANSITIVE VERB When you **boil** food, or when it **boils**, it is cooked in boiling water.

○ She boiled the beans to soften their skins.

○ I peeled potatoes and put them in water to boil.

boiled /bɔɪld/

FOOD AND DRINK: COOKING

ADJECTIVE **Boiled** food is food cooked in boiling water.

○ The lamb is served with boiled potatoes and vegetables.

○ Boiled lobsters are prepared by dropping them in boiling water when they are alive.

boiled egg /bɔɪld ɛg/ (boiled eggs)

FOOD AND DRINK: BREAKFAST

NOUN A **boiled egg** is an egg cooked in boiling water.

○ Do you prefer fried or boiled eggs?

○ She wanted boiled eggs so I put two eggs in a pan of water.

> **OTHER WAYS OF SERVING EGGS**
>
> The following are other ways of cooking and serving eggs:
>
> fried egg, hard-boiled egg, omelet, poached egg, scrambled egg, soft-boiled egg

bot|tled beer /bɒtəld bɪər/ (bottled beers)

FOOD AND DRINK: ALCOHOLIC DRINKS

COUNT/NONCOUNT NOUN **Bottled beer** is beer that is sold in a bottle.

○ The bar has a range of draft and bottled beers.

○ We have draft beer and lots of bottled beers too.

bot|tle top /bɒtᵊl tɒp/ (bottle tops)

HOTEL BAR

NOUN A **bottle top** is a small cover, usually made of metal, that seals a bottle.

○ Remove the bottle top from the bottle and place it on the table.

○ To open the bottle, place the bottle opener over the bottle top.

bran|dy /brændi/ (brandies)

FOOD AND DRINK: ALCOHOLIC DRINKS

COUNT/NONCOUNT NOUN **Brandy** is a strong alcoholic drink. A **brandy** is often drunk after a meal.

○ Always offer guests a brandy after dinner.

○ They have a glass of brandy after their evening meal.

bread /brɛd/

FOOD AND DRINK: BREAKFAST

NOUN **Bread** is a very common food made from flour, water, and usually yeast.

○ He wants a ham and salad sandwich on brown bread.

○ We bake our own bread using good quality flour.

bread bas|ket /brɛd bæskɪt/ (bread baskets)

FOOD AND DRINK: DINING

NOUN A **bread basket** is a basket for carrying or holding bread or bread rolls.

○ He took a slice of bread from the bread basket on the table.

○ Serve bread and large crusty rolls in the bread basket.

bread plate /brɛd pleɪt/ (bread plates)

RESTAURANT: EQUIPMENT

NOUN A **bread plate** is a small plate for bread that you eat along with your main meal.

B

○ The bread plate is on the left of the dinner plate.

○ Put bread plates beside the dinner plates for the customers to have bread with their meals.

▶ **SYNONYM:**
side plate

---

break|fast and din|ner (in BRIT use **half board**) /brɛkfəst ən dɪnər/

RESERVATIONS AND CHECKING IN AND OUT

NOUN **Breakfast and dinner** is a system of accommodations in a hotel or guest house, in which you pay for a room and breakfast and dinner the following day.

○ The break consists of three nights' accommodation with breakfast and dinner.

○ Breakfast and dinner are included in your stay; you only have to get your own lunch.

---

bring the check (in BRIT use **bring the bill**) /brɪŋ ðə tʃɛk/
(**brings the check, brought the check, bringing the check**)

RESTAURANT: PAYING THE CHECK

PHRASE If you **bring the check** in a restaurant, you bring the customer a piece of paper on which the price of their meal is written.

○ Bring the check when the customer asks for it at the end of the meal.

○ Bring the check to the customer on a small tray, with the check face down.

---

bro|chure /broʊʃʊər/ (**brochures**)

GENERAL

NOUN A **brochure** is a thin magazine with pictures that gives you information about a product or service.

○ Full details of our charges are contained in the brochure available at reception.

○ Let me get you some brochures. These will give you an idea of what is available in the hotel.

buf|fet line /bʊfeɪ laɪn/ (buffet lines)

RESTAURANT

NOUN A **buffet line** is a selection of food that is displayed on a long table. Guests usually serve themselves.

○ *Place silverware and napkins at the end of the buffet line.*

○ *Put desserts on the buffet line for guests to serve themselves after the main course is cleared.*

> **PRONUNCIATION**
>
> Note the silent "t" in the word "buffet."

---

bunk beds /bʌŋk bɛdz/

HOTEL ROOM: BEDROOM

NOUN **Bunk beds** are two beds that are attached to each other, one above the other, in a frame.

○ *The family room includes a double bed and bunk beds for children.*

○ *Younger guests enjoy climbing the ladder to the top bunk of the bunk beds.*

---

bus boy /bʌs bɔɪ/ (bus boys)

RESTAURANT: PERSONNEL

NOUN A **bus boy** is someone whose job is to set or clear tables in a restaurant.

○ *A bus boy cleared the plates and the waitress brought fresh glasses.*

○ *He got a job as a bus boy clearing tables in a fashionable restaurant.*

▶ **SYNONYM:**
busser

---

busi|ness cen|ter /bɪznɪs sɛntər/

HOTEL FACILITIES

NOUN A **business center** is a room in a hotel with facilities such as computers and a fax machine, that allows guests to work while they are staying at the hotel.

○ The hotel's business center offers a wide range of services for the corporate traveler.

○ Business travelers appreciate the staffed business center, which allows them to use the hotel as an office.

---

bus|ser /bʌsər/ (bussers)

RESTAURANT: PERSONNEL

NOUN A **busser** is someone whose job is to set or clear tables in a restaurant.

○ The busser ensures that all the tables are clean.

○ Restaurants usually employ a busser to clear all the tables.

▶ **SYNONYM:**
  bus boy

---

but|ter /bʌtər/

FOOD AND DRINK: BREAKFAST

NOUN **Butter** is a soft yellow substance made from cream. You spread it on bread or use it in cooking.

○ The waiter brought some butter along with the bread.

○ Put bread, and butter for the bread, on the bread plate.

---

but|ter knife /bʌtər naɪf/ (butter knives)

RESTAURANT: EQUIPMENT

NOUN A **butter knife** is a blunt knife that you use to cut and spread butter.

○ Place the butter knife next to the butter on the table.

○ The butter knife can be placed on the bread and butter plate.

Cc

cab|bage /kæbɪdʒ/

FOOD AND DRINK: VEGETABLES

NOUN **Cabbage** is a round vegetable with white, green, or purple leaves that is usually eaten cooked.

○ Steam or boil the cabbage until it is tender.

○ Cook the cabbage in salted water for five minutes.

ca|la|ma|ri /kæləmɑrɪ/

FOOD AND DRINK: FISH AND SEAFOOD

NOUN **Calamari** is pieces of squid cooked for eating, usually cut into rings and fried in batter.

○ Calamari is made with squid.

○ The seafood plate has fresh prawns, oysters, and calamari.

can|cel a res|er|va|tion /kænsəl ə rɛzərveɪʃən/ (cancels a reservation, canceled a reservation, canceling a reservation)

RESERVATIONS AND CHECKING IN AND OUT

PHRASE If you **cancel a reservation**, you stop it because someone who has booked a room has informed you that they no longer wish to stay there.

○ We canceled the customer's reservation because her travel plans had changed.

○ If you cancel your reservation early you will receive a full refund of your deposit.

C

can|cel|la|tion dead|line /kænsᵊleɪʃᵊn dɛdlaɪn/
(**cancellation deadlines**)

RESERVATIONS AND CHECKING IN AND OUT

NOUN A **cancellation deadline** is a date before which you must cancel a hotel reservation without paying any money.

○ You may cancel your reservation up until the cancellation deadline shown on your booking.

○ If you cancel your reservation after the cancellation deadline, you will have to pay for one night's stay.

can|cel|la|tion fee /kænsᵊleɪʃᵊn fi/ (**cancellation fees**)

RESERVATIONS AND CHECKING IN AND OUT

NOUN A **cancellation fee** is a sum of money you must pay if you cancel a hotel reservation after the cancellation deadline.

○ The hotel will not charge any cancellation fees if you cancel your reservation up to two weeks in advance.

○ A cancellation fee will be charged according to the number of days' notice you give of the cancellation.

car|pet /kɑrpɪt/ (**carpets**)

HOTEL ROOM: BEDROOM

NOUN A **carpet** is a thick covering of soft material which is laid over a floor or a staircase.

○ Push back furniture and vacuum the carpet to pick up dirt.

○ The hotel has laid new carpets on the stairs as part of its refurbishment.

▶ COLLOCATION:
fitted carpet

car|rot /kærət/ (**carrots**)

FOOD AND DRINK: VEGETABLES

NOUN **Carrots** are long, thin, orange-colored vegetables.

○ The salad contains lettuce, tomatoes, carrots, and onions.

○ The ham is served with a colorful blend of orange carrots and green peas.

carve /kɑrv/ (carves, carved, carving)

FOOD AND DRINK: COOKING

TRANSITIVE/INTRANSITIVE VERB If you **carve** a piece of cooked meat, you cut slices from it so that you can eat it.

○ *Carve the breast from the bone and serve with eggplant and sauce.*

○ *I will carve the turkey into slices for the evening meals.*

cas|se|role /kæsəroʊl/ (casseroles)

FOOD AND DRINK: MEAT

NOUN A **casserole** is a dish made of meat and vegetables that have been cooked slowly in a liquid.

○ *Try the lamb and potato casserole.*

○ *I put the beef and vegetables into a casserole and cooked it slowly.*

cau|li|flow|er /kɔliflaʊər/

FOOD AND DRINK: VEGETABLES

NOUN **Cauliflower** is a large, round vegetable that has a hard, white center surrounded by green leaves.

○ *Wash the cauliflower and remove the outer leaves.*

○ *Break the hard center of the cauliflower into segments.*

cel|er|y /sɛləri/

FOOD AND DRINK: VEGETABLES

NOUN **Celery** is a vegetable with long, pale green stalks. It is eaten raw in salads.

○ *Chop an onion and a stick of celery for the salad.*

○ *Serve the dip with sticks cut from carrots and celery stalks.*

▶ **COLLOCATION:**
stick of celery

c

ce|re|als /sɪəriəlz/

FOOD AND DRINK: BREAKFAST

NOUN **Cereals** are foods made from grain. They are mixed with milk and eaten for breakfast.

○ *The hotel offers a free breakfast with cereal, orange juice, and coffee.*

○ *The breakfast buffet includes cereals made from wheat, corn, and rice.*

> **RELATED WORDS**
>
> Compare **cereal** with **granola**, which is a breakfast cereal usually consisting of oats, wheat germ, sesame seeds, and dried fruit or nuts.

chair /tʃɛər/ (chairs)

RESTAURANT: EQUIPMENT

NOUN A **chair** is a piece of furniture for one person to sit on, with a back and four legs.

○ *We arranged five chairs around each table.*

○ *I put the chairs back beside the tables in the dining room.*

cham|ber|maid /tʃeɪmbərmeɪd/ (chambermaids)

HOTEL PERSONNEL

NOUN A **chambermaid** is a woman who cleans the bedrooms in a hotel.

○ *The chambermaid's duty is to clean guest rooms and other parts of the hotel.*

○ *They were hired as chambermaids, cleaning rooms at a fashionable hotel.*

cham|pagne /ʃæmpeɪn/

FOOD AND DRINK: ALCOHOLIC DRINKS

NOUN **Champagne** is an expensive French white wine with bubbles in. It is often drunk to celebrate something.

○ *Because it was a special occasion, she opened a bottle of champagne and poured everyone a glass.*

○ *We offer newly married guests a complimentary bottle of champagne to celebrate.*

▶ **COLLOCATION:**
glass of champagne

---

cham|pagne buck|et /ʃæmpeɪn bʌkɪt/ (**champagne buckets**)

RESTAURANT: EQUIPMENT

NOUN A **champagne bucket** is a container that holds ice cubes or cold water and ice. You can use it to put bottles of champagne in and keep the champagne cool.

○ *Place the bottle in a champagne bucket with water and ice cubes.*

○ *The champagne bucket contains three bottles of champagne.*

---

change a res|er|va|tion /tʃeɪndʒ ə rɛzərveɪʃ°n/ (**changes a reservation, changed a reservation, changing a reservation**)

RESERVATIONS AND CHECKING IN AND OUT

PHRASE If you **change a reservation**, you move a booking to a different date because someone who has booked a room has informed you that they wish to stay there on a different date.

○ *You may change your reservation by calling at least 72 hours before your check-in.*

○ *The guest's flight has been cancelled – can we change the reservation so he can check in tomorrow?*

---

change the sheets /tʃeɪndʒ ðə ʃɪts/ (**changes the sheets, changed the sheets, changing the sheets**)

HOUSEKEEPING AND MAINTENANCE

PHRASE If you **change the sheets** on a bed, you take the used sheets off the bed and put on different ones.

○ *The chambermaid changed the sheets on the bed.*

○ *How often do you change the sheets on the beds in the rooms?*

chan|nel /tʃænəl/ (channels)

HOTEL ROOM: BEDROOM

NOUN A **channel** is a television station.

○ The TV has a remote control to change the channel and volume.

○ The number of channels available on the television was limited.

▶ SYNONYM:
station

▶ COLLOCATION:
change channel

charge to a room /tʃɑrdʒ tu ə rum/ (charges to a room, charged to a room, charging to a room)

RESTAURANT: PAYING THE CHECK

PHRASE If you **charge** an item or expense **to a room** at a hotel, you add it to a guest's final bill so they can pay for it when they check out of the room.

○ The restaurant offers meals which can be charged to your room.

○ Any items that you charged to your room during your stay must be paid for when you check out.

check¹ (in BRIT use **bill**) /tʃɛk/ (checks)

RESTAURANT: PAYING THE CHECK

NOUN The **check** in a restaurant is a piece of paper on which the price of your meal is written and which you are given before you pay.

○ Do you want coffee or do you want the check right away?

○ When the time came to pay for the meal, she asked for the check.

check² (BRIT **cheque**) /tʃɛk/ (checks)

RESTAURANT: PAYING THE CHECK

NOUN A **check** is a printed form on which you write an amount of money and who it is to be paid to. Your bank then pays the money to that person from your account.

○ *Does the hotel accept checks?*

○ *You can also pay for bookings by card, cash, or check.*

---

check in /tʃɛk ɪn/ (**checks in, checked in, checking in**)

RESERVATIONS AND CHECKING IN AND OUT

VERB When you **check in** to a hotel, or if someone checks you in, you arrive and go through the necessary procedures before you stay there.

○ *He called the hotel to tell them they will check in tomorrow.*

○ *The woman who checked him in asked if he would like to have dinner in the hotel restaurant.*

---

check-in time /tʃɛk ɪn taɪm/ (**check-in times**)

RESERVATIONS AND CHECKING IN AND OUT

NOUN The **check-in time** at a hotel is the time from which guests are expected to arrive.

○ *Check-in time is from 3pm on your day of arrival.*

○ *At all our hotels there is no latest check-in time, so you can arrive when you like.*

---

check out /tʃɛk aʊt/ (**checks out, checked out, checking out**)

RESERVATIONS AND CHECKING IN AND OUT

VERB When you **check out** of a hotel where you have been staying, or if someone checks you out, you pay the bill and leave.

○ *They packed and checked out of the hotel.*

○ *There is a 24-hour reception service so guests can check in or check out at any time.*

C

check-out time /tʃɛk aʊt taɪm/ (check-out times)

RESERVATIONS AND CHECKING IN AND OUT

NOUN The **check-out time** at a hotel is the time by which guests are expected to leave.

○ If you require a later check-out time, please inform reception before 10am.

○ Check-out times are usually between 11am and 12 noon on the day of departure.

chef /ʃɛf/ (chefs)

RESTAURANT: PERSONNEL

NOUN A **chef** is a cook in a restaurant or hotel.

○ Our chef is famous for her delicious cooking.

○ The talented chefs in the restaurant can prepare a variety of dishes.

cher|ry /tʃɛri/ (cherries)

FOOD AND DRINK: FRUIT

NOUN **Cherries** are small, round fruit with red skins.

○ The pie is made with fresh red cherries and sugar.

○ Sweet red cherries should be small and not too firm.

▶ COLLOCATIONS:
cherry pie
cherry stone

chick|en /tʃɪkɪn/

FOOD AND DRINK: MEAT

NOUN **Chicken** is the flesh of a type of bird which is kept on a farm for its eggs and for its meat, eaten as food.

○ Choose from roast chicken, grilled steaks, and pork fillets.

○ Chicken needs slightly longer to cook than other birds such as duck and goose.

▶ COLLOCATIONS:
chicken wing
fried chicken
roast chicken

chop /tʃɒp/ (chops, chopped, chopping)

FOOD AND DRINK: MEAT

VERB If you **chop** food, you cut it into pieces with strong, downward movements of a knife.

○ Chop the butter into small pieces.

○ Finely chop the onions and garlic with a sharp knife.

clam /klæm/ (clams)

FOOD AND DRINK: FISH AND SEAFOOD

NOUN **Clams** are a kind of shellfish which can be eaten.

○ The fish is served with mussels and clams out of their shells.

○ Pick the clams from the shells and place them in a bowl.

clean a room /klin ə rum/ (cleans a room, cleaned a room, cleaning a room)

HOUSEKEEPING AND MAINTENANCE

PHRASE If you **clean a room**, you make the inside of it and the furniture in it free from dirt and dust.

○ A maid will clean your room.

○ She worked as a chambermaid and cleaned hotel rooms.

RELATED WORDS

The following are also housekeeping terms that relate to cleaning a room:

change the sheets
to take the used sheets off a bed and put on different ones

dust
to remove dust from furniture usually using a cloth

empty the wastebasket
to remove the contents of a small container for paper garbage and put them in the trash

polish
to put a substance on something and rub it with a cloth to make it shine

service a room
to clean and change the towels and bed linen in a room

sweep
to push dirt or garbage off an area of floor or ground using a
brush with a long handle

vacuum
to clean a floor or carpet using a piece of electrical equipment
that sucks up dirt

---

clear a ta|ble /klɪər ə teɪbᵊl/ (clears a table, cleared a table, clearing a table)

FOOD AND DRINK: DINING

PHRASE When you **clear a table**, you remove things from it that you
do not want to be there.

○ I cleared the table after dinner.

○ Are you still eating your meal, or may I clear the table?

---

clos|et /klɒzɪt/ (closets)

HOTEL ROOM: BEDROOM

NOUN A **closet** is a very small room for storing things, especially one
without windows.

○ The closet in the suite is large, with plenty of room for clothes.

○ Fetch the pan and brush from the broom closet.

---

cloth /klɒθ/ (cloths)

HOUSEKEEPING AND MAINTENANCE

NOUN A **cloth** is a piece of cloth which you use for a particular
purpose, such as cleaning something or covering something.

○ Dust surfaces in all rooms with a damp cloth.

○ The waiter spread a new cloth on the table.

cock|tail /kɒkteɪl/ (cocktails)

HOTEL BAR

NOUN A **cocktail** is an alcoholic drink which contains several ingredients.

○ On arrival, guests are offered champagne cocktails.

○ The bar serves delicious cocktails made from brandy and cream.

▶ COLLOCATIONS:
champagne cocktail
cocktail party

cock|tail shak|er /kɒkteɪl ʃeɪkər/ (cocktail shakers)

HOTEL BAR

NOUN A **cocktail shaker** is a metal container for mixing ingredients to make cocktails.

○ Shake the ingredients together in a cocktail shaker.

○ Fill a cocktail shaker with ice and add the juice of a lemon.

cof|fee /kɒfi/ (coffees)

FOOD AND DRINK: BREAKFAST

COUNT/NONCOUNT NOUN **Coffee** is a hot drink made with water and ground or powdered coffee beans.

○ Would you like decaffeinated coffee?

○ Would you like a coffee, tea, or other hot drink?

▶ COLLOCATIONS:
black coffee
cup of coffee
fresh coffee

cog|nac /koʊnyæk/ (cognacs)

FOOD AND DRINK: ALCOHOLIC DRINKS

COUNT/NONCOUNT NOUN **Cognac** is a type of brandy made in the southwest of France.

○ He served the customer with some vintage cognac.

○ He prefers cognac to any other brandy.

cold cuts /koʊld kʌts/

FOOD AND DRINK: MEAT

NOUN **Cold cuts** are thin slices of cooked meat which are served cold.

○ The main course includes cold cuts such as chicken, roast beef, and salami.

○ Our customers have fresh cold cuts of beef and ham every day.

cold meat /koʊld miːt/ (**cold meats**)

FOOD AND DRINK: MEAT

COUNT/NONCOUNT NOUN **Cold meat** is cooked meat that is served cold.

○ The dining room offers a selection of salad dishes with cold meats such as turkey and ham.

○ The supper is a buffet and there is plenty of cold chicken and other cold meat.

cole|slaw /koʊlslɔ/

FOOD AND DRINK: VEGETABLES

NOUN **Coleslaw** is a salad of chopped raw cabbage, carrots, onions, and sometimes other vegetables, usually with mayonnaise.

○ The coleslaw is made with red cabbage rather than white.

○ There is too much mayonnaise in this coleslaw.

com|fort|er /kʌmfərtər/ (**comforters**)

HOTEL ROOM: BEDROOM

NOUN A **comforter** is a large cover filled with feathers or similar material that you use like a blanket.

○ All rooms have air-conditioning, as well as down comforters.

○ Crisp sheets and fluffy comforters are on the beds.

▶ SYNONYMS:
  duvet
  quilt

---

comp /kɒmp/ (comps, comped, comping)

RESERVATIONS AND CHECKING IN AND OUT

VERB If a place such as a hotel or a restaurant **comps** you, or if they **comp** you **to** something, they give you a room or a meal without charging you for it.

  ○ *The manager came to the table to apologize and let us know our bill would be comped.*

  ○ *His ice cream was free because the waitress comped him to it.*

---

com|plain a|bout the food /kəmpleɪn əbaʊt ðə fud/
(complains about the food, complained about the food, complaining about the food)

FOOD AND DRINK: DINING

VERB If you **complain about the food**, you say that you are not satisfied with it.

  ○ *Restaurants refund money to customers who complain about the food.*

  ○ *Many guests complain about the food when they are not satisfied with it.*

---

com|plaint /kəmpleɪnt/ (complaints)

RESERVATIONS AND CHECKING IN AND OUT

NOUN A **complaint** is a statement in which you express your dissatisfaction with a situation.

  ○ *There have been a number of complaints about the standard of service.*

  ○ *If you wish to make a written complaint, send this to the manager.*

▶ COLLOCATION:
  make a complaint

C

> **TALKING ABOUT COMPLAINTS**
>
> If you **make** a complaint, you complain about something.
>
> If you **have**, **get**, or **receive** a complaint, someone complains to you about something for which you are responsible.

con|ci|erge /kɒnsiɛɜrʒ/ (concierges)

HOTEL PERSONNEL

NOUN A **concierge** is an employee of a hotel who assists guests.

○ When I asked for the key to the room, the concierge handed me several messages.

○ The concierge can help guests to book restaurants and taxis.

con|fer|ence fa|cil|i|ties /kɒnfərəns fəsɪlɪtiz/

HOTEL FACILITIES

NOUN **Conference facilities** are large rooms and pieces of equipment that a hotel provides so an organization can have a conference there.

○ The modern conference facilities include a large conference hall seating 80 people.

○ Conference facilities are available for large business meetings of up to 400 people.

con|fer|ence room /kɒnfərəns rum/ (conference rooms)

HOTEL FACILITIES

NOUN A **conference room** is a large room in a hotel where a number of people can have a conference.

○ The conference room has eight seats and two tables.

○ There are three conference rooms, each of which is equipped with a large screen for business presentations.

con|firm a res|er|va|tion /kənfɜrm ə rɛzərveɪʃᵊn/
(**confirms a reservation, confirmed a reservation, confirming a reservation**)

FOOD AND DRINK: DINING

PHRASE If you **confirm a reservation**, you inform someone who has booked a room at a hotel that the reservation is definite.

○ *He phoned the hotel the day before he arrived to confirm the reservation.*

○ *A written reservation and deposit is required to confirm your reservation at the hotel.*

con|ti|nen|tal break|fast /kɒntɪnɛntᵊl brɛkfəst/
(**continental breakfasts**)

FOOD AND DRINK: BREAKFAST

NOUN A **continental breakfast** is breakfast that consists of food such as bread, butter, jam, and a hot drink. There is no cooked food.

○ *There is a continental breakfast with cereal, croissants, butter, and jelly.*

○ *There is a choice of cooked breakfast or continental breakfast which can be served in your room.*

> **RELATED WORDS**
>
> Compare **continental breakfast** with **English breakfast**, which is a breakfast that consists of cooked food such as bacon, eggs, and pancakes.

cook¹ /kʊk/ (**cooks**)

FOOD AND DRINK: COOKING

NOUN A **cook** is a person whose job is to prepare and cook food, for example in a restaurant or hotel.

○ *The cook prepares and serves breakfast, snacks, and one main meal per day.*

○ *Our cooks provide food that is well prepared.*

c

cook² /kʊk/ (cooks, cooked, cooking)

FOOD AND DRINK: COOKING

TRANSITIVE/INTRANSITIVE VERB When you **cook** food, or when food **cooks**, it is heated until it is ready to be eaten.

○ *Cook the vegetables gently for about ten minutes.*

○ *We cook our tuna steaks by frying or grilling.*

cork /kɔrk/ (corks)

HOTEL BAR

NOUN A **cork** is a piece of cork or plastic that is pushed into the opening of a bottle to close it.

○ *A waitperson takes the cork from the bottle and presents the wine.*

○ *He took out the cork and offered her the bottle.*

cork|screw /kɔrkskru/ (corkscrews)

HOTEL BAR

NOUN A **corkscrew** is a device for pulling corks out of bottles.

○ *She fetched the corkscrew for the wine and two glasses.*

○ *The bartender removed the cork from the bottle with a corkscrew.*

cor|po|rate rate /kɔrpərɪt reɪt/ (corporate rates)

RESERVATIONS AND CHECKING IN AND OUT

NOUN A **corporate rate** is the amount of money a hotel charges guests who are staying there because they are traveling for business reasons. It is usually less than the normal amount.

○ *Corporate rates for business guests are $199 a night Monday to Friday and $109 on weekends.*

○ *If you regularly stay at the hotel on business, you can pay the special corporate rate.*

cor|ri|dor /kɔ́rɪdər/ (corridors)

HOTEL FACILITIES

NOUN A **corridor** is a long passage in a building, with doors and rooms on one or both sides.

○ There are doors on both sides of the corridor.

○ I ran down the corridor towards the elevator.

cou|pon /kúpɒn/ (coupons)

RESERVATIONS AND CHECKING IN AND OUT

NOUN A **coupon** is a piece of printed paper which allows you to pay less money than usual for a product, or to get it free.

○ With the coupon, you get an entrée free.

○ Please present this coupon at check-in to receive the special rate.

cov|er charge /kʌ́vər tʃɑrdʒ/ (cover charges)

RESTAURANT: PAYING THE CHECK

NOUN A **cover charge** is a sum of money that you must pay in some restaurants in addition to the money that you pay there for your food and drink.

○ Restaurants may add a $2 per person cover charge to your meal.

○ In addition to the cost of food and drinks, there is a cover charge of 10% on the final bill.

RELATED WORDS

Compare **cover charge** with **discretionary service charge**, which is an amount that is added to your check in a restaurant which you can choose to pay or not pay.

C

C

cred|it card guar|an|tee / krɛdɪt kɑrd gærənti/ (credit card guarantees)

RESERVATIONS AND CHECKING IN AND OUT

NOUN If you pay for a booking at a hotel by credit card, a **credit card guarantee** allows the hotel to charge a cost to your credit card if you do not arrive on the day you arranged or if you damage something in the hotel.

○ Reservations at the hotel require one night's deposit or credit card guarantee.

○ If you are not able to give a credit card guarantee, the room must be paid in advance.

cred|it card ter|mi|nal /krɛdɪt kɑrd tɜrmɪnᵊl/ (credit card terminals)

RESTAURANT: PAYING THE CHECK

NOUN A **credit card terminal** is a piece of equipment that you use to read the information on a credit card and charge a cost to it.

○ You need a credit card terminal to process credit card payments.

○ Fetch the credit card terminal and then swipe the card.

crib /krɪb/ (cribs)

RESTAURANT: PAYING THE CHECK

NOUN A **crib** is a bed for a baby.

○ Does the hotel provide cribs for babies?

○ We provide cribs and high chairs for infants at no extra charge.

crois|sant /krwɑsɑ̃/ (croissants)

FOOD AND DRINK: BREAKFAST

NOUN **Croissants** are small, sweet bread rolls in the shape of a crescent that are eaten for breakfast.

○ Fresh-baked croissants are served with breakfast.

○ She prefers sweet croissants to other bread rolls.

cup /kʌp/ (cups)

RESTAURANT: EQUIPMENT

NOUN A **cup** is a small round container that you drink from. Cups usually have handles and are made from china or plastic.

○ She put the cups and saucers for the tea on the tables.

○ Can I get you a small cup of coffee?

▶ **COLLOCATION:**
  cup and saucer

cush|ion /kʊʃⁿn/ (cushions)

HOTEL ROOM: BEDROOM

NOUN A **cushion** is a fabric case filled with soft material, which you put on a seat to make it more comfortable.

○ The chair and sofa have large comfortable cushions.

○ I arranged some soft cushions on the chairs.

Dd

dai|ly news|pa|per /deɪli nuzpeɪpər/ (**daily newspapers**)

RESERVATIONS AND CHECKING IN AND OUT

NOUN A **daily newspaper** is a newspaper that is published every day of the week except Sunday.

○ Free daily newspapers are delivered to your hotel room every day.

○ If you would like a daily newspaper to catch up with the news, we will provide one.

Dan|ish pas|try /deɪnɪʃ peɪstri/ (**Danish pastries**)

FOOD AND DRINK: BREAKFAST

NOUN **Danish pastries** are cakes made from sweet pastry. They are often filled with things such as apple or almond paste.

○ The waitress brought them two coffees and two apricot Danish pastries.

○ We offered chocolate croissants and almond Danish pastries from a tray.

---

de|caf|fein|at|ed cof|fee /diːkæfɪneɪtɪd kɔfi/
(**decaffeinated coffees**)

FOOD AND DRINK: BREAKFAST

COUNT/NONCOUNT NOUN **Decaffeinated coffee** is coffee that does not contain caffeine.

○ He wants a cup of decaffeinated coffee and a cup of regular coffee.

○ I'm afraid we don't have decaffeinated coffee – we only have regular coffee.

de|duct from the bill (BRIT) /dɪdʌkt frəm ðə bɪl/ (deducts from the bill, deducted from the bill, deducting from the bill)

RESERVATIONS AND CHECKING IN AND OUT

PHRASE If you **deduct** an item or expense **from the bill** at a restaurant or hotel, you take a charge out of a customer's bill.

○ If you are not happy with the meal, ask the manager to deduct the cost from the bill.

○ Your deposit will be deducted from your bill on the day you check out.

deep-fried /diːp fraɪd/

FOOD AND DRINK: COOKING

ADJECTIVE **Deep-fried** food is food cooked in a deep pan that contains a large amount of fat or oil.

○ They ordered deep-fried chicken and chips.

○ To make deep-fried chicken, put the pieces in a deep pan of hot oil.

de|par|ture date /dɪpɑːtʃər deɪt/ (departure dates)

RESERVATIONS AND CHECKING IN AND OUT

NOUN Your **departure date** is the date that you are expected to leave a hotel or other location.

○ Rooms must be vacated by 12am on the agreed departure date.

○ You will be asked to confirm your departure date so the receptionist knows when you will check out.

de|pos|it /dɪpɒzɪt/ (deposits)

RESERVATIONS AND CHECKING IN AND OUT

NOUN A **deposit** is a sum of money which you pay when you book a room at a hotel or guest house. The amount is taken off your final bill when you leave.

○ Most hotel owners ask for a deposit to confirm a reservation.

○ If you cancel your reservation more than 60 days before your arrival date, then we will refund your deposit.

▶ COLLOCATIONS:
ask for a deposit
lose one's deposit

---

des|sert /dɪzɜrt/ (desserts)

FOOD AND DRINK: DINING

NOUN A **dessert** is something sweet, such as fruit, pastry, or ice cream, that you eat at the end of a meal.

○ They ordered pavlova for dessert.

○ For dessert he ordered chocolate cake.

▶ SYNONYM:
pudding

---

des|sert bowl /dɪzɜrt boʊl/ (dessert bowls)

RESTAURANT: EQUIPMENT

NOUN A **dessert bowl** is a bowl in which a dessert is served.

○ Spoon the apples into dessert bowls.

○ These dessert bowls are perfect for single servings of ice cream.

---

des|sert men|u /dɪzɜrt mɛnyu/ (dessert menus)

RESTAURANT: EQUIPMENT

NOUN In a restaurant or café, the **dessert menu** is a list of the desserts that are available.

○ The dessert menu includes sorbets and ice creams.

○ Choose your favorite dessert from the dessert menu.

---

des|sert spoon /dɪzɜrt spun/ (dessert spoons)

RESTAURANT: EQUIPMENT

NOUN A **dessert spoon** is a spoon which is midway between the size of a teaspoon and a tablespoon. You use it to eat desserts.

○ Place the dessert spoon near the dessert bowls.

○ Bring out the dessert bowls and dessert spoons after the entrée.

des|sert wine /dɪzɜrt waɪn/ (dessert wines)

FOOD AND DRINK: ALCOHOLIC DRINKS

COUNT/NONCOUNT NOUN A **dessert wine** is a sweet wine, usually a white wine, that is served with dessert.

○ There is a list of four dessert wines to accompany your dessert, served by the glass or bottle.

○ Dessert wine can be served without a dessert, but it tastes better with a dessert.

> **TYPES OF WINE**
>
> The following are other types of wine:
>
> champagne, dry white wine, dry wine, medium dry white wine, red wine, rosé wine, sparkling wine, white wine

di|ges|tif /diʒɛstif/ (digestifs)

RESTAURANT: EQUIPMENT

NOUN A **digestif** is a drink that you have before or after a meal to help you digest the food.

○ Order a digestif in the drawing room to finish your meal.

○ Brandy and port are popular digestifs to serve after meals.

> **RELATED WORDS**
>
> Compare **digestif** with **aperitif** which is an alcoholic drink that you have before a meal.

din|ner plate /dɪnər pleɪt/ (dinner plates)

RESTAURANT: EQUIPMENT

NOUN A **dinner plate** is a plate on which a large meal is served.

○ They set the dinner plates on the counter to serve the main course.

○ The waitperson brought the dinner plates and side plates to the table.

dis|count /dɪskaʊnt/ (discounts)

RESERVATIONS AND CHECKING IN AND OUT

NOUN A **discount** is a reduction in the usual price of something.

○ *Local restaurants offer discounts for dining early.*

○ *All full-time staff get a 20 percent discount on meals.*

dis|cre|tion|ar|y ser|vice charge /dɪskrɛʃənɛri sɜrvɪs tʃɑrdʒ/ (discretionary service charges)

RESTAURANT: PAYING THE CHECK

NOUN A **discretionary service charge** is an amount that is added to your bill in a restaurant to pay for the work of the person who comes and serves you. You can decide if you want to pay it.

○ *A discretionary service charge may be added to your check to reward good service.*

○ *We add a discretionary service charge of 12%, which goes completely to the staff.*

dock|ing sta|tion /dɒkɪŋ steɪʃən/ (docking stations)

HOTEL ROOM: BEDROOM

NOUN A **docking station** is a device that connects a portable electronic device to a fixed power supply.

○ *Amenities in the room include phone, alarm clock, and iPod docking station.*

○ *Recharge all your gadgets with the docking station in your room.*

do not dis|turb sign /duː nɒt dɪstɜrb saɪn/ (do not disturb signs)

HOTEL ROOM: BEDROOM

NOUN A **do not disturb sign** is a sign that a guest in a hotel hangs outside their room to tell other people not to knock the door or enter.

○ *Your cleaner will enter your room daily, unless the do not disturb sign is on the outside door handle.*

○ *They left the room at 11:00 am and removed the do not disturb sign from the door.*

door chain /dɔr tʃeɪn/ (**door chains**)

HOTEL ROOM: BEDROOM

NOUN A **door chain** is a small chain, attached to the inside of a door, which you can attach to the frame of the door to cover the opening for extra security.

○ Use the door chain when opening your door.

○ When they went to bed they put the door chain across the room door.

door han|dle /dɔr hændəl/ (**door handles**)

HOTEL ROOM: BEDROOM

NOUN A **door handle** is a small round object or a lever that is attached to a door and is used for opening and closing it.

○ I turned the door handle and found the door was open.

○ The door handle is broken so I can't open the door.

door|man /dɔrmæn/ (**doormen**)

HOTEL PERSONNEL

NOUN A **doorman** is a person, usually a uniformed employee, who stands at the door of a building such as a hotel and helps people who are going in or out.

○ The doorman held open the door for the guest as they entered the hotel.

○ The doorman opened the door and helped the guest into a cab.

dou|ble bed /dʌbəl bɛd/ (**double beds**)

HOTEL ROOM: BEDROOM

NOUN A **double bed** is a bed that is wide enough for two people to sleep in.

○ One room has a king-sized double bed and the others single beds.

○ You can choose between a double bed or two single beds.

d

D

dou|ble meas|ure /dʌbᵊl mɛʒər/ (double measures)

HOTEL ROOM: BEDROOM

NOUN A **double measure** is a drink that is twice the normal measure.

○ *All our spirits are double measures. Single measures are available.*

○ *Do you want a single or a double measure of brandy?*

dou|ble room /dʌbᵊl rum/ (double rooms)

HOTEL ROOM: BEDROOM

NOUN A **double room** is a room intended for two people, usually a couple, to stay in.

○ *One person occupying a double room has to pay a supplement.*

○ *She needs two double rooms for four guests.*

drain (in BRIT use plughole) /dreɪn/ (drains)

HOTEL ROOM: BATHROOM

NOUN A **drain** is a hole in a bathtub or sink that allows the water to flow away.

○ *The shower drain is blocked with hair.*

○ *The stopper for the drain of the sink is missing.*

drapes (in BRIT use curtains) /dreɪps/

HOTEL ROOM: BEDROOM

NOUN **Drapes** are long heavy curtains.

○ *She opened the drapes to let in the light.*

○ *There were no blinds or drapes at the windows on the lower floors.*

▶ **COLLOCATIONS:**
close the drapes
open the drapes

drawers /drɔːz/

HOTEL ROOM: BEDROOM

NOUN **Drawers** are parts of a desk, chest, or other piece of furniture that are shaped like a box and are designed for putting things in. You pull them toward you to open them.

○ The drawers of the desk are jammed.

○ Two of the drawers in the chest of drawers are missing.

dry white wine /draɪ waɪt waɪn/ (**dry white wines**)

FOOD AND DRINK: ALCOHOLIC DRINKS

COUNT/NONCOUNT NOUN **Dry white wine** is white wine that does not have a sweet taste.

○ Would you prefer a medium or dry white wine?

○ Dinner was fish, accompanied by a glass of a pale and crisp dry white wine.

dry wine /draɪ waɪn/ (**dry wines**)

FOOD AND DRINK: ALCOHOLIC DRINKS

COUNT/NONCOUNT NOUN **Dry wine** is wine that does not have a sweet taste.

○ This is a dry wine, not a sweet dessert wine.

○ I always prefer a dry wine with savory food and a sweet wine with dessert.

duck /dʌk/

FOOD AND DRINK: MEAT

NOUN **Duck** is the flesh of a type of water bird, eaten as food.

○ Poultry dishes such as chicken, duck, and turkey are very popular.

○ We serve gourmet poultry meals, including duck, turkey, and goose.

dust /dʌst/ (dusts, dusted, dusting)

[HOUSEKEEPING AND MAINTENANCE]

TRANSITIVE/INTRANSITIVE VERB When you **dust** something such as furniture or a room, you remove dust from it, usually using a cloth.

○ The chambermaid dusted all the furniture in the room.

○ Every day I dust the furniture with a cloth to remove all the dust and crumbs.

dust|er /dʌstər/ (dusters)

[HOUSEKEEPING AND MAINTENANCE]

NOUN A **duster** is a cloth which you use for removing dust from furniture, ornaments, or other objects.

○ Give the counter a clean with a soft duster.

○ Wipe the tables with a duster to remove all the dust.

du|ty man|ag|er /duti mænɪdʒər/ (duty managers)

[HOTEL PERSONNEL]

NOUN A **duty manager** is a person who is in charge at a particular time.

○ Ask to speak to the duty manager who will be pleased to help you.

○ When I complained, the duty manager who was managing that day didn't apologize.

du|vet /duveɪ/ (duvets)

[HOTEL ROOM: BEDROOM]

NOUN A **duvet** is a large cover filled with feathers or similar material that you use like a blanket.

○ You can choose between a duvet and sheets on the bed.

○ The duvets on the beds were lumpy and thin, so he asked for a woolen blanket.

du|vet cov|er /duveɪ kʌvər/ (**duvet covers**)

| HOTEL ROOM: BEDROOM |

NOUN A **duvet cover** is a large piece of fabric which you put a duvet inside in order to protect it.

○ *The duvet cover was too big for the duvet.*

○ *I'll have to change the duvet covers on the duvets.*

Ee

ear|ly check-in /ˈɜrli tʃɛk ɪn/ (early check-ins)

HOTEL ROOM: BEDROOM

COUNT/NONCOUNT NOUN An **early check-in** at a hotel is an arrangement which allows a guest to check in earlier than the normal time.

○ Early check-in (before 11.00am) is possible by arrangement if guests inform the hotel in advance.

○ I am arriving early. How do I request an early check-in at the hotel?

eggs /ɛgz/

FOOD AND DRINK: BREAKFAST

NOUN In many countries, **eggs** often means hen's eggs, eaten as food.

○ I ordered fried eggs but got boiled eggs with breakfast.

○ You can have your eggs over easy or sunny side up.

el|e|va|tor (in BRIT use **lift**) /ˈɛlɪveɪtər/ (elevators)

HOTEL FACILITIES

NOUN An **elevator** is a device that carries people or goods up and down inside tall buildings.

○ We took the elevator to the fourteenth floor.

○ The elevators are used by the staff for taking sheets and towels down to another level.

▶ COLLOCATION:
take the elevator

emp|ty the waste|bas|ket /ɛmpti ðə weɪstbæskɪt/
(empties the wastebasket, emptied the wastebasket, emptying the wastebasket)

PHRASE If you **empty the wastebasket**, you remove its contents and put them in the trash.

○ Cleaners in this hotel empty wastebaskets, dust, and vacuum.

○ I cleaned the rooms and emptied the wastebaskets to get rid of the trash.

Eng|lish break|fast /ɪŋglɪʃ brɛkfəst/ (English breakfasts)

FOOD AND DRINK: BREAKFAST

NOUN An **English breakfast** is breakfast that consists of cooked food such as bacon, eggs, and pancakes.

○ An English breakfast is too large for me. I prefer to have just fruit and cereal.

○ We provide seven large English breakfasts and five dinners each week.

en|trée /ɒntreɪ/ (entrées)

FOOD AND DRINK: DINING

NOUN At restaurants or formal dinners, the **entrée** is the main course, or sometimes a dish before the main course.

○ Dinner features a hot entrée of chicken, veal, or lamb.

○ There is a selection of appetizers followed by an entrée.

▶ **SYNONYM:**
main course

es|ca|lope /ɪskɑləp/ (escalopes)

FOOD AND DRINK: MEAT

NOUN An **escalope** is a thin slice of meat or fish without a bone.

○ The next course is escalopes of salmon.

○ Put four escalopes of the fish, without bones, on each plate.

e|vac|u|a|tion route /ɪˌvæyuˈeɪʃ⁰n ˈrut/ (evacuation routes)

HOTEL FACILITIES

NOUN An **evacuation route** is a way to get out of a building if there is an emergency, such as a fire.

○ A clear evacuation route is very important if there is a fire.

○ In an emergency, the main evacuation route is through the front door.

e|vent /ɪˈvɛnt/ (events)

GENERAL

NOUN An **event** is a planned and organized occasion, for example a social gathering.

○ The hotel can hold events such as wedding receptions, parties, and conferences.

○ Our hotels can host large events and we can cater for all your needs.

▶ **COLLOCATIONS:**
hold an event
host an event

ex|pi|ra|tion date /ˌɛkspəˈreɪʃ⁰n ˈdeɪt/ (expiration dates)

RESERVATIONS AND CHECKING IN AND OUT

NOUN The **expiration date** of a credit card is the date, written on the card, when it stops being valid.

○ We need your credit card number and expiration date.

○ Your credit card must have an expiration date that is after your check-out date.

Ff

fa|cil|i|ties /fəsɪlɪtiz/

HOTEL FACILITIES

NOUN **Facilities** are buildings, pieces of equipment, or services that are provided for a particular purpose.

○ Hotels may charge for the use of leisure facilities such as swimming pools and gyms.

○ What recreational facilities are available in the hotel?

fau|cet (in BRIT use **tap**) /fɔsɪt/ (**faucets**)

HOTEL ROOM: BATHROOM

NOUN A **faucet** is a device that controls the flow of a liquid or gas from a pipe or container. Sinks and baths have faucets attached to them.

○ I went into the bathroom and turned on the faucets to fill the tub.

○ Clean both the faucets on the basin.

▶ **COLLOCATIONS:**
turn off the faucet
turn on the faucet

fax¹ /fæks/ (**faxes**)

HOTEL FACILITIES: BUSINESS CENTER

NOUN A **fax** is a copy of a document that is transmitted electronically along a telephone line by a fax machine.

○ You can book by phone or send a fax.

○ Is there a fax machine to send faxes from this hotel?

F

fax² /fæks/ (faxes, faxed, faxing)

HOTEL FACILITIES: BUSINESS CENTER

VERB If you **fax** a document to someone, you send it from one fax machine to another.

○ I faxed a copy of the reservation to each of the guests.

○ Did you mail or fax the guest a confirmation of her reservation?

feath|er pil|low /fɛðər pɪloʊ/ (feather pillows)

HOTEL ROOM: BEDROOM

NOUN A **feather pillow** is a soft piece of cloth, filled with feathers, used to rest your head on in bed.

○ The bed is comfortable, and we have both feather pillows and regular pillows.

○ You can have feather pillows or pillows with artificial fillings.

feed|back form /fidbæk fɔrm/ (feedback forms)

HOTEL ROOM: BEDROOM

NOUN A **feedback form** is a paper with questions on it and spaces marked where you should write the answers. It asks a hotel guest if they enjoyed their stay and what could be improved.

○ Please tell us where we can improve our service on the feedback form.

○ To give your feedback please either e-mail us or fill in the feedback form.

fil|let¹ /fɪleɪ/

FOOD AND DRINK: MEAT

NOUN A **fillet** is a strip of meat or fish that has no bones in it.

○ She ordered the fillet of beef and found bones in it.

○ Trim the beef fillets and remove any bones.

fil|let² /fɪleɪ/ (fillets, filleted, filleting)

FOOD AND DRINK: MEAT

VERB When you **fillet** fish or meat, you prepare it by taking the bones out.

○ *Fillet the fish and roll the fillets in flour.*

○ *I fillet the chicken by cutting it off the bone.*

---

fire door /faɪər dɔr/ (fire doors)

HOTEL FACILITIES

NOUN A **fire door** is a door inside a building which is closed to prevent a fire from spreading.

○ *Fire doors must always be kept shut.*

○ *People sometimes wedge open fire doors in hotels, and this is dangerous if there is a fire.*

---

fire es|cape /faɪər ɪskeɪp/ (fire escapes)

HOTEL FACILITIES

NOUN A **fire escape** is a metal staircase on the outside of a building, which can be used to escape from the building if there is a fire.

○ *There is a fire escape outside the kitchen window that should be used in the event of a fire.*

○ *Guests must be able to locate the evacuation route and the fire escape in the event of an emergency.*

> **RELATED WORDS**
>
> Compare **fire escape** with **evacuation route**, which is a way to get out of a building if there is an emergency, such as a fire.

---

fire ex|tin|guish|er /faɪər ɪkstɪŋgwɪʃər/ (fire extinguishers)

HOTEL EQUIPMENT

NOUN A **fire extinguisher** is a metal cylinder which contains water or chemicals at high pressure which can put out fires.

○ *Notices give details of how to evacuate and where to find fire extinguishers in the event of a fire.*

○ *The hotel has fire doors, a fire alarm, and fire extinguishers to put out any fires.*

first sit|ting /fɜrst sɪtɪŋ/ (first sittings)

HOTEL EQUIPMENT

NOUN A **first sitting** is the first period when a meal is served if there is not enough space for everyone to eat at the same time.

○ You can have the first sitting of dinner at 6:30 or the second sitting after 8:30.

○ There are two sittings for dinner, with the first sitting at 6:00.

fish course /fɪʃ kɔrs/ (fish courses)

HOTEL EQUIPMENT

NOUN A **fish course** is a part of a meal in which fish is served, usually before the entrée.

○ Tuna was served for the fish course.

○ The fish course was a thick steak of smoked salmon.

fish knife /fɪʃ naɪf/ (fish knives)

RESTAURANT: EQUIPMENT

NOUN A **fish knife** is a knife that you use when you eat fish. It has a wide flat blade and does not have a sharp edge.

○ The restaurant provided fish knives when fish was served.

○ He asked for a regular knife for the fish course and not a fish knife.

fit|ness cen|ter /fɪtnɪs sɛntər/ (fitness centers)

HOTEL EQUIPMENT

NOUN A **fitness center** in a hotel is a large room, usually containing special equipment, where people go to do physical exercise and get fit.

○ The hotel's fitness center includes a new gym.

○ You can keep fit during your stay in the hotel's fitness center.

fix /fɪks/ (fixes, fixed, fixing)

HOUSEKEEPING AND MAINTENANCE

VERB If you **fix** something which is damaged or which does not work properly, you repair it.

○ *While they were fixing the leak, we had no water.*

○ *When will you fix the broken elevator?*

fixed-price men|u /fɪkst praɪs mɛnyu/ (fixed-price menus)

FOOD AND DRINK: DINING

NOUN In a restaurant, the cost of a meal on a **fixed-price menu** stays the same and does not vary.

○ *Many restaurants offer the option of a fixed-price menu as well as à la carte.*

○ *The restaurant offers a fixed-price menu at lunchtime, so you know what you will have to pay.*

flat-screen tel|e|vi|sion /flæt skrin tɛlɪvɪʒᵊn/ (flat-screen televisions)

HOTEL ROOM: BEDROOM

NOUN A **flat-screen television** is a television with a flat, narrow screen.

○ *All rooms have flat-screen televisions with digital channels.*

○ *The hotel has replaced the old type of television in the rooms with new flat-screen televisions.*

flat|ware (in BRIT use **cutlery**) /flætwɛər/

RESTAURANT: EQUIPMENT

NOUN You can refer to the knives, forks, and spoons that you eat your food with as **flatware**.

○ *Put the flatware (knives, forks and spoons) away in the drawers.*

○ *Remove used dishes and flatware from the tables after the meal.*

flo|rist /flɔrɪst/ (florists)

[HOTEL FACILITIES]

NOUN A **florist** is a shopkeeper who arranges and sells flowers and sells house plants.

○ The hotel's florist can create floral arrangements for all occasions.

○ The florist provides flowers for weddings and other events.

food and bev|er|age man|ag|er /fud ən bɛvərɪdʒ mænɪdʒər/ (food and beverage managers)

[HOTEL PERSONNEL]

NOUN A **food and beverage manager** is responsible for providing food and drink for the guests at a hotel or restaurant.

○ We need a food and beverage manager to run the hotel restaurant, bar, and kitchen.

○ The job of food and beverage manager includes planning menus and hiring cooks.

fork /fɔrk/ (forks)

[RESTAURANT: EQUIPMENT]

NOUN A **fork** is a tool used for eating food which has a row of three or four long metal points at the end.

○ Three forks were laid to go with the three knives.

○ Bring a clean knife and fork for the next course.

four-course meal /fɔr kɔrs mil/ (four-course meals)

[FOOD AND DRINK: DINING]

NOUN A **four-course meal** is a meal that consists of four parts served one after the other.

○ The restaurant is offering two-course, three-course, and four-course meals with table service.

○ The four-course meal consists of a soup, an appetizer, an entrée, and dessert.

freeze /friːz/ (freezes, froze, frozen, freezing)

FOOD AND DRINK: COOKING

VERB If you **freeze** something such as food, you preserve it by storing it at a temperature below freezing point.

○ *Freeze the extra sauce to preserve it for later.*

○ *Find out how to freeze, thaw, and reheat foods safely.*

French fries (in BRIT use **chips**) /frɛntʃ fraɪz/

FOOD AND DRINK: VEGETABLES

NOUN **French fries** are long, thin pieces of potato fried in oil or fat.

○ *The French fries were thin and crispy.*

○ *To cook the French fries, put them into a deep pan of oil.*

fresh|ly squeezed /frɛʃli skwiːzd/

FOOD AND DRINK: BREAKFAST

ADJECTIVE You can describe juice that has been recently pressed out of fruit as **freshly squeezed**.

○ *They asked for freshly squeezed carrot juice and toast.*

○ *The hotel offers a breakfast of homemade biscuits, freshly squeezed orange juice and coffee.*

▶ **COLLOCATION:**
freshly squeezed juice

fried /fraɪd/

FOOD AND DRINK: COOKING

ADJECTIVE **Fried** food is food cooked in a pan that contains hot fat or oil.

○ *Our fried foods are cooked in olive oil.*

○ *To make the fried prawns, cook them in a shallow pan of oil with garlic and chilli.*

> **RELATED WORDS**
>
> Compare **fried** with **deep-fried**, which means cooked in a deep
> pan that contains a large amount of fat or oil.
>
> o *deep-fried prawns*

fried egg /fraɪd ɛg/ (fried eggs)

FOOD AND DRINK: BREAKFAST

NOUN A **fried egg** is an egg cooked in oil or fat.

o *Would you like your fried eggs over easy?*

o *To make fried eggs, put a small amount of oil in a pan and crack the eggs
into it.*

fried po|ta|to /fraɪd pəteɪtoʊ/ (fried potatoes)

FOOD AND DRINK: VEGETABLES

NOUN **Fried potatoes** are pieces of potato cooked in oil or fat.

o *Main meals come with your choice of boiled or fried potatoes.*

o *Fried potatoes are better when the potatoes are cooked in duck fat.*

front of house man|ag|er /frʌnt əv haʊs mænɪdʒər/
(front of house managers)

HOTEL PERSONNEL

NOUN A **front of house manager** is responsible for the reception and
reservations at a hotel.

o *On the first floor, you will be greeted by the front of house manager.*

o *The front of house manager looks after the reception area.*

fro|zen /froʊzᵊn/

FOOD AND DRINK: COOKING

ADJECTIVE **Frozen** food has been preserved by being kept at a very low
temperature.

○ *Frozen yoghurt is a healthy alternative to ice cream.*

○ *Most frozen food must be defrosted before it is cooked.*

> **RELATED WORDS**
>
> The opposite of **frozen** is **fresh**.
>
> ○ *fresh fruit/vegetables*

---

fruit juice /frut dʒus/ (fruit juices)

FOOD AND DRINK: BREAKFAST

COUNT/NONCOUNT NOUN **Fruit juice** is the liquid that can be obtained from a fruit. Fruit juice is often drunk at breakfast.

○ *Fruit juices include apple, grape, orange, and pineapple.*

○ *The fruit juices we serve are freshly squeezed from the fruit.*

---

fry /fraɪ/ (fries, fried, frying)

FOOD AND DRINK: COOKING

VERB When you **fry** food, you cook it in a pan that contains hot fat or oil.

○ *Gently fry the sausages in a pan with oil.*

○ *Fry the breadcrumbs in the hot fat until they are golden brown.*

---

ful|ly booked /fʊli bʊkt/

RESERVATIONS AND CHECKING IN AND OUT

ADJECTIVE If a hotel or restaurant is **fully booked**, it has no rooms or tables left for a particular time or date.

○ *Sorry, the hotel is fully booked. Please try the hotel across the road.*

○ *The hotel was fully booked, but we've just had a cancellation so a room is free now.*

func|tion /fʌŋkʃ°n/ (functions)

GENERAL

NOUN A **function** is a large formal dinner or party.

○ *The hotel added a ballroom to cater for functions and weddings.*

○ *Our hotel is ideal for hosting your wedding celebration or other function.*

▶ **COLLOCATIONS:**
hold a function
host a function

func|tion room /fʌŋkʃ°n rum/ (function rooms)

GENERAL

NOUN A **function room** is a large room where formal dinners or parties can be held.

○ *The function room is ideal for business conferences and special occasions.*

○ *The function room has a modern sound system and a bar.*

fur|ni|ture pol|ish /fɜrnɪtʃər pɒlɪʃ/

HOUSEKEEPING AND MAINTENANCE

NOUN **Furniture polish** is a substance that you put on the surface of a piece of furniture in order to clean it and make it shine.

○ *I cleaned and polished the table with furniture polish.*

○ *Use furniture polish to shine your wood and furniture.*

Gg

game /geɪm/

FOOD AND DRINK: MEAT

NOUN Wild animals or birds that are hunted for sport and sometimes cooked and eaten are referred to as **game**.

○ They serve game such as pheasant and pigeon.

○ Game is more flavorful than farmed meats such as chicken and pork.

gar|lic /gɑrlɪk/

FOOD AND DRINK: VEGETABLES

NOUN **Garlic** is the small, white, round bulb of a plant that is related to the onion plant. Garlic has a very strong smell and taste and is used in cooking.

○ We use garlic to add a very strong flavor to the food.

○ If you don't want a strong taste of garlic, add one clove instead of two.

▶ **COLLOCATION:**
clove of garlic

gen|er|al man|ag|er /dʒɛnərəl mænɪdʒər/ (**general managers**)

HOTEL PERSONNEL

NOUN A **general manager** of a hotel is a person who has overall responsibility for the management of the hotel.

○ The general manager has responsibility for the running of the hotel.

○ The general manager conducts all the staff interviews.

gher|kin /ɡɜrkɪn/ (gherkins)

FOOD AND DRINK: VEGETABLES

NOUN **Gherkins** are small green cucumbers that have been preserved in vinegar.

○ Gherkins are kept in jars of vinegar.

○ The fish is garnished with small green gherkins, pickled onions, and mustard.

G

glass¹ /ɡlæs/ (glasses)

HOTEL ROOM: BATHROOM

NOUN A **glass** is a container made from glass, which you can drink from and which does not have a handle.

○ The waiter filled all the glasses on the table with water.

○ All our drinks are served in large glasses.

> **TYPES OF GLASS**
>
> The following are all types of glass with a particular function:
>
> **beer glass**
> a glass, usually with no stem, which you use for drinking beer
>
> **shot glass**
> a small glass without a stem which you use for drinking small amounts of a strong alcoholic drink
>
> **wine glass**
> a glass, usually with a narrow stem, which you use for drinking wine

glass² /ɡlæs/ (glasses)

HOTEL ROOM: BATHROOM

NOUN The contents of a glass can be referred to as a **glass of** something.

○ Can I have a sandwich and a glass of milk, please?

○ Would you like a large glass or a small glass of juice?

goose /guːs/

FOOD AND DRINK: MEAT

NOUN **Goose** is the flesh of a type of bird which is often kept on a farm for its meat, eaten as food.

○ The main dish that day was roast goose.

○ Goose can be cooked in the same way as other poultry.

grab han|dle /græb hændªl/ (grab handles)

HOTEL ROOM: BATHROOM

NOUN A **grab handle** is a handle on the side of an object such as a bathtub that you hold in order to help you get in and out.

○ There are grab handles to get in and out of the tub.

○ The accessible room has lower beds and grab handles in the bathroom.

gra|no|la /grənoʊlə/

FOOD AND DRINK: BREAKFAST

NOUN **Granola** is a breakfast cereal usually consisting of oats, wheatgerm, sesame seeds, and dried fruit or nuts.

○ There is granola and two other cereal choices.

○ Our granola is made from oats and wheat, bound together with honey.

▶ **SYNONYM:**
muesli

grape /greɪp/ (grapes)

FOOD AND DRINK: FRUIT

NOUN **Grapes** are small green or purple fruit which grow in bunches. Grapes can be eaten raw, used for making wine, or dried.

○ Put a bunch of grapes in the bowl.

○ He took two apples and a bunch of grapes from the fruit tray.

▶ **COLLOCATION:**
bunch of grapes

grape|fruit /ɡreɪpfrut/ (grapefruits)

FOOD AND DRINK: FRUIT

COUNT/NONCOUNT NOUN A **grapefruit** is a large, round, yellow fruit, similar to an orange, that has a sharp, slightly bitter taste.

○ I find grapefruit too bitter to eat. I prefer oranges.

○ Would you like orange juice or grapefruit juice with your breakfast?

gra|tu|i|ty /ɡrətuɪti/ (gratuities)

RESTAURANT: PAYING THE CHECK

NOUN A **gratuity** is a gift of money to someone who has done something for you.

○ The porter expects a gratuity.

○ Most people add a 15% gratuity to the bill for the waiter.

▶ **COLLOCATION:**
give a gratuity

guest re|la|tions man|ag|er /ɡɛst rileɪʃənz mænɪdʒər/ (guest relations managers)

RESTAURANT: PAYING THE CHECK

NOUN A **guest relations manager** at a hotel is responsible for the relationships that the hotel has with its guests and the way in which it treats them.

○ Our guest relations manager will assist you with any requests you have.

○ When I checked out, the guest relations manager asked if I enjoyed my stay.

guest ser|vic|es /ɡɛst sɜrvɪsɪz/

HOTEL FACILITIES

NOUN **Guest services** at a hotel are the services, amenities and help that the hotel provides for its guests.

○ Guest services include free morning orange juice and newspaper delivery.

○ Tickets for local shows are available to guests at the guest services desk in the lobby.

guest ser|vic|es man|ag|er /gɛst sɜrvɪsɪz mænɪdʒər/
(guest services managers)

RESTAURANT: PAYING THE CHECK

NOUN A **guest services manager** at a hotel is responsible for the services and facilities that the hotel provides for its guests.

○ *The guest services manager will help you enjoy your stay.*

○ *The guest services manager is responsible for the employees who provide services for guests.*

g

gym /dʒɪm/ **(gyms)**

HOTEL FACILITIES

NOUN A **gym** is a large room, usually containing special equipment, where people go to do physical exercise and get fit.

○ *The gym has exercise bikes and running machines.*

○ *While some guests play golf, others work out in the hotel gym.*

Hh

hair|dress|er /hɛərdrɛsər/ (hairdressers)

HOTEL FACILITIES

NOUN A **hairdresser** is a person who cuts, colors, and arranges people's hair.

○ Visit the hairdresser in the hotel for a quick trim.

○ Our in-house hairdresser styles hair for both ladies and gentlemen.

hair|dry|er /hɛər draɪər/ (hairdryers)

HOTEL ROOM: BEDROOM

NOUN A **hairdryer** is a machine that you use to dry your hair.

○ There is a wall socket for a hairdryer in the bedroom.

○ If you are going to wash your hair, you can borrow a hairdryer from reception.

hall /hɔl/ (halls)

HOTEL FACILITIES

NOUN A **hall** in a building is a long passage with doors into rooms on both sides of it.

○ There are ten rooms along each hall.

○ The lights were on in the hall and in the guest bedrooms.

ham /hæm/

FOOD AND DRINK: MEAT

NOUN **Ham** is meat from the top of the back leg of a pig, specially treated so that it can be kept for a long period of time.

○ *The ham in the sandwich was thinly sliced.*

○ *The ham from a pig's leg is often not as lean as bacon.*

▶ **COLLOCATION:**
slice of ham

---

hand tow|el /hænd taʊəl/ (**hand towels**)

HOTEL ROOM: BATHROOM

NOUN A **hand towel** is a small towel used for drying your hands.

○ *The hand towel is the smallest towel provided in the room.*

○ *Provide two hand towels and two bath towels in each bathroom.*

h

---

hang|er /hæŋər/ (**hangers**)

HOTEL ROOM: BEDROOM

NOUN A **hanger** is a curved piece of wood, metal, or plastic that you hang a piece of clothing on.

○ *There are no hangers in the closet.*

○ *We provide plenty of hangers in the wardrobes for guests' clothes.*

---

hap|py hour /hæpi aʊər/ (**happy hours**)

HOTEL BAR

NOUN In a bar, **happy hour** is a period when drinks are sold more cheaply than usual to encourage people to come to the bar.

○ *Don't forget happy hour 7–9pm, when all drinks are half price.*

○ *During happy hour a pint of beer is cheaper than usual.*

---

hard-boiled egg /hɑrd bɔɪld ɛg/ (**hard-boiled eggs**)

HOTEL BAR

NOUN A **hard-boiled egg** has been boiled in its shell until the whole of the inside is solid.

○ *Do you prefer hard-boiled eggs or soft-boiled?*

○ *It is easier to peel the shell from a hard-boiled egg when it is cool.*

hash browns /hæʃ braʊnz/

FOOD AND DRINK: BREAKFAST

NOUN **Hash browns** or **hashed browns** are potatoes that have been chopped into small pieces, formed into small cakes, and cooked on a grill or in a frying pan.

○ *There are two ways of making hash browns, using raw or cooked potatoes.*

○ *Our hash browns are freshly made from chopped and grilled potatoes.*

H

head wait|er /hɛd weɪtər/ (head waiters)

HOTEL BAR

NOUN A **head waiter** is in charge of the other waiters in a restaurant.

○ *The head waiter is in charge of all waiting staff.*

○ *The head waiter of the restaurant looked around to see who needed service.*

health club /hɛlθ klʌb/ (health clubs)

HOTEL BAR

NOUN A **health club** in a hotel is a facility that people go to in order to do exercise and have beauty treatments.

○ *The health clubs in our hotels are full of modern exercise equipment.*

○ *Our health club features a pool, gym, and Jacuzzi, all available for guests to use.*

hold a res|er|va|tion /hoʊld ə rɛzərveɪʃⁿn/ (holds a reservation, held a reservation, holding a reservation)

RESERVATIONS AND CHECKING IN AND OUT

PHRASE If a hotel **holds a reservation**, it keeps a room for someone, and does not give it to someone else.

○ *Many hotels require a credit card to hold a reservation.*

○ *If you would like us to hold a reservation for you, call the reservations manager to confirm your arrival date.*

hors d'oeu|vres /ɔr dɜrvz/

RESTAURANT

NOUN **Hors d'oeuvres** are small amounts of food served before the main course of a meal.

- ○ Take the tray of hors d'oeuvres out for the guests after they have been seated.

- ○ The waitress put the platter of hors d'oeuvres down in the dining room before the main meal.

> **PRONUNCIATION**
>
> Note the French pronunciation: ɔr dɜrvz. The "h" is silent.

h

---

host /houst/ (hosts)

RESTAURANT: PERSONNEL

NOUN The **host** of a hotel is a person who has overall responsibility for the way the hotel operates.

- ○ As the host, he has overall responsibility for the way the hotel operates.
- ○ The host will wait for you in reception and give you the keys to your room.

---

host an e|vent /houst ən ɪvɛnt/ (hosts an event, hosted an event, hosting an event)

HOTEL FACILITIES

PHRASE If a hotel or organization **hosts an event**, it provides the facilities for the event to take place.

- ○ Throughout the year, the hotel hosts special events.
- ○ Events can be hosted in the hotel's conference rooms.

---

host|ess /houstɪs/ (hostesses)

RESTAURANT: PERSONNEL

NOUN The **hostess** of a hotel is a woman who has overall responsibility for the way the hotel operates.

○ *As the hostess, she has overall responsibility for the way the hotel operates.*

○ *The hostess is often the first person a hotel guest meets.*

---

ho|tel li|mo /houtɛl lɪmoʊ/ (hotel limos)

HOTEL ROOM: BATHROOM

NOUN A **hotel limo** is a large and very comfortable car. Hotel limos usually have a driver and are hired to bring guests to and from the hotel.

○ *The doorman met me when I got out of the hotel limo.*

○ *There is a hotel limo service to the hotel from the airport.*

---

ho|tel li|mo driv|er /houtɛl lɪmoʊ draɪvər/ (hotel limo drivers)

HOTEL ROOM: BATHROOM

NOUN A **hotel limo driver** is the person whose job it is to drive the hotel limo.

○ *The hotel limo driver collects you at the airport.*

○ *The hotel limo driver will call you when he is at reception and collect you in the limo.*

---

hot tub /hɒt tʌb/ (hot tubs)

HOTEL ROOM: BATHROOM

NOUN A **hot tub** is a very large, round bath which several people can sit in together.

○ *Guests can soak in a relaxing hot tub in the leisure center.*

○ *Relax in the Jacuzzi or with your friends in the hot tub on the terrace.*

---

house|keep|er /haʊskipər/ (housekeepers)

HOTEL PERSONNEL

NOUN A **housekeeper** is a person whose job is to clean and take care of hotel rooms.

○ *The housekeeper checks all the rooms to be cleaned.*

○ The housekeeper has the key to the linen closet and gives the bedding to the maids.

---

house|keep|ing /ˈhaʊskiːpɪŋ/

GENERAL

NOUN **Housekeeping** is the service in a hotel that cleans and maintains the rooms.

○ The resorts offer room service and daily housekeeping.

○ Ask housekeeping to clear your room when you go out.

---

house|keep|ing cart /ˈhaʊskiːpɪŋ kɑːrt/ (**housekeeping carts**)

HOTEL PERSONNEL

NOUN A **housekeeping cart** is a large metal basket on wheels which is used by a cleaner in a hotel to move clean bed linen, towels, and cleaning equipment.

○ We took clean towels off the housekeeping cart in the hall.

○ It is difficult to move the housekeeping cart down the corridor.

h

Ii

ice /aɪs/

HOTEL BAR

NOUN Ice is pieces of frozen water that you put in drinks to keep them cool.

- I went to the refrigerator for more ice.
- Could we have long drinks with lots of ice please?

ice buck|et /aɪs bʌkɪt/ (ice buckets)

HOTEL ROOM: BEDROOM

NOUN An **ice bucket** is a container that holds ice cubes or cold water and ice. You can use it to provide ice cubes to put in drinks, or to put bottles of wine in and keep the wine cool.

- Bring a bottle of wine in an ice bucket.
- Fill an ice bucket with ice if the customer ordered a white wine.

ice cream /aɪs kriːm/

FOOD AND DRINK: DINING

NOUN Ice cream is a very cold sweet food made from frozen cream or a substance like cream and has a flavor such as vanilla, chocolate, or strawberry.

- What flavor of ice cream do you prefer?
- Do you want ice cream for dessert?

ice cu|be /aɪs kyub/ (ice cubes)

FOOD AND DRINK: DINING

NOUN An **ice cube** is a small square block of ice that you put into a drink in order to make it cold.

○ He dropped three ice cubes into a glass and poured a drink.

○ Use ice cubes to keep a drink cool.

ice ma|chine /aɪs məʃin/

HOTEL ROOM: BEDROOM

NOUN An **ice machine** is a machine that produces ice to put in drinks.

○ Plenty of ice is available for our guests from the ice machines.

○ Is there an ice machine on each floor if I need ice?

▶ SYNONYM:
ice dispenser

in|ci|den|tal charg|es /ɪnsɪdɛntᵊl tʃɑrdʒɪz/

RESERVATIONS AND CHECKING IN AND OUT

NOUN **Incidental charges** are costs of items and services that are not part of the main bill.

○ You must give a credit card to cover any incidental charges such as phone calls and room service.

○ Payment for accommodation and incidental charges must be made when checking out.

in|clud|ed /ɪnkludɪd/

RESERVATIONS AND CHECKING IN AND OUT

ADJECTIVE You use **included** to emphasize that an item or service is part of an overall cost.

○ It costs $350 per person for five nights, all meals included.

○ You can have seven meals per week, drinks included.

---

in|spect /ɪnspɛkt/ (inspects, inspected, inspecting)

HOUSEKEEPING AND MAINTENANCE

VERB When an official **inspects** a hotel or restaurant, they visit it and check it carefully, for example, in order to find out whether regulations are being obeyed.

○ Health officials inspect the hotel once a year.

○ Tourism officials arrived to inspect the hotel rooms.

---

in-suite din|ing /ɪn swit daɪnɪŋ/

HOTEL FACILITIES

NOUN **In-suite dining** in a hotel is when guests eat meals in their rooms.

○ The hotel offers a full restaurant menu for in-suite dining if you do not want to visit the restaurant.

○ The in-suite dining service is only served until 11pm.

In|ter|net ac|cess /ɪntərnɛt æksɛs/

HOTEL FACILITIES

NOUN If you have **Internet access**, you have facilities to use the Internet.

○ Most hotels have business centers with computers for Internet access, but they can be expensive.

○ We are pleased to offer our guests complimentary Internet access on our computers.

Ja|cuz|zi /dʒəkˈuːzɪ/ (Jacuzzis)

HOTEL ROOM: BATHROOM

NOUN A **Jacuzzi** is a large circular bath which is fitted with a device that makes the water move around.

○ *The luxury hotel offers a Jacuzzi in every bathroom.*

○ *After a busy day your Jacuzzi is the best place to relax.*

jel|ly (in BRIT use **jam**) /dʒˈɛli/

FOOD AND DRINK: BREAKFAST

NOUN **Jelly** is a sweet food that is made by cooking fruit or fruit juice with a large amount of sugar until it is thickened. It is usually spread on bread.

○ *He had two peanut butter and jelly sandwiches.*

○ *At breakfast time, you can have a fruit jelly for your toast or bagel.*

j

Kk

---

key card /ki kɑrd/ (key cards)

HOTEL EQUIPMENT

NOUN A **key card** is a small plastic card which you can use instead of a key to open a door.

○ The electronic key card to her room does not work.

○ Put the key card in the slot outside the door.

---

king-sized bed /kɪŋ saɪzd bɛd/ (king-sized beds)

HOTEL ROOM: BEDROOM

NOUN A **king-sized bed** is a bed that is the largest size available.

○ All double rooms have king-sized beds.

○ The double rooms have a comfortable king-sized bed.

> **RELATED WORDS**
>
> Compare **king-sized bed** with **queen-sized bed** which is a bed that is smaller than a king-sized bed but larger than a double bed.

---

ki|wi fruit /kiwi frut/ (kiwi fruits)

FOOD AND DRINK: FRUIT

NOUN A **kiwi fruit** is a fruit with a brown hairy skin and green flesh.

○ The dish includes exotic fruit such as kiwi fruit and mango.

○ A box of pineapple, kiwi fruit, and melon was delivered.

knife /naɪf/ (knives)

RESTAURANT: EQUIPMENT

NOUN A **knife** is a tool for cutting and consists of a flat piece of metal with a sharp edge on the end of a handle.

○ *She asked a waiter to replace her knife and fork.*

○ *Place the knives on the right hand side of the plates.*

k

Ll

lamb /læm/

FOOD AND DRINK: MEAT

NOUN **Lamb** is the flesh of a lamb eaten as food.

○ *The lamb was tender and the bread was fresh.*

○ *Leg of lamb is easier to carve than other cuts.*

▶ COLLOCATIONS:
lamb chop
leg of lamb
rack of lamb

lan|gous|tine /lɒŋgustin/ (langoustines)

FOOD AND DRINK: FISH AND SEAFOOD

NOUN **Langoustines** are large prawns or small lobsters, eaten as food.

○ *The seafood restaurant offers fresh oysters, langoustines, and grilled fish.*

○ *Whole langoustines are included in our seafood platters.*

late check-out /leɪt tʃɛk aʊt/ (late check-outs)

RESERVATIONS AND CHECKING IN AND OUT

COUNT/NONCOUNT NOUN A **late check-out** at a hotel is an arrangement which allows a guest to check out later than the normal time.

○ *There is a late check-out at noon.*

○ *If you wish to leave later, you can buy a late check-out at the time of booking.*

laun|dry bag /ˈlɔndri bæg/ (**laundry bags**)

RESERVATIONS AND CHECKING IN AND OUT

NOUN A **laundry bag** is a bag for clothes that are about to be washed.

○ Keep soiled clothes separate in a plastic laundry bag.

○ The hotel will wash one laundry bag of clothes for $10.

laun|dry ser|vice /ˈlɔndri sɜrvɪs/ (**laundry services**)

HOTEL FACILITIES

NOUN A **laundry service** is a service in a hotel that washes and irons clothes for guests.

○ Almost all hotels have a laundry service. If you hand in clothes one day you should get them back a day or two later.

○ The laundry service will wash, dry, and iron your clothes.

leave feed|back /ˈliv ˈfidbæk/ (**leaves feedback, left feedback, leaving feedback**)

GENERAL

PHRASE If a guest **leaves feedback**, they tell you if they enjoyed their stay and what could be improved.

○ Please leave feedback about your stay using the form provided.

○ Thank you for taking the time to leave feedback about our hotel.

lem|on /ˈlɛmən/ (**lemons**)

FOOD AND DRINK: FRUIT

COUNT/NONCOUNT NOUN A **lemon** is a bright yellow fruit with very sour juice.

○ Serve mineral water with ice and lemon.

○ Would you like a slice of lemon in your drink?

▶ **COLLOCATION:**
slice of lemon

lend /lɛnd/ (**lends, lent, lending**)

GENERAL

VERB If you **lend** something, you allow someone to have it or use it for a period of time.

○ Hostels and hotels often lend bicycles to guests.

○ If you need a hairdryer, ask our reception staff and they will lend you one.

RELATED WORDS

A related word is **borrow**, which means to take something from someone else and use it for a period of time.

○ I'm sure you could borrow a hairdryer from reception.

○ I'm sure reception will lend you a hairdryer.

---

let|tuce /lɛtɪs/ (**lettuces**)

FOOD AND DRINK: VEGETABLES

COUNT/NONCOUNT NOUN A **lettuce** is a plant with large green leaves that is the basic ingredient of many salads.

○ All salads include lettuce.

○ Place two lettuce leaves on each plate.

▶ COLLOCATION:
lettuce leaf

---

li|a|bil|i|ty /laɪəbɪlɪti/

GENERAL

NOUN **Liability** is legal responsibility for something.

○ The hotel does not accept liability for valuable items.

○ Does the hotel have liability if something is stolen?

▶ COLLOCATIONS:
accept liability
liability for

lime /laɪm/ (limes)

FOOD AND DRINK: FRUIT

COUNT/NONCOUNT NOUN A **lime** is a green fruit that tastes like a lemon.

○ *The customer wants a slice of lime in his drink.*

○ *Cooks use lime and other citrus fruits to add taste to dishes.*

▶ **COLLOCATION:**
slice of lime

---

line (in BRIT use **queue**) /laɪn/ (lines)

RESERVATIONS AND CHECKING IN AND OUT

NOUN A **line** of people is a number of them that are waiting one behind another, for example, in order to check in to a hotel.

○ *We had to wait as there was a long line for the restaurant.*

○ *You will have to join the line to check in.*

---

liq|uor /lɪkər/

FOOD AND DRINK: ALCOHOLIC DRINKS

NOUN Strong alcoholic drinks such as whiskey, vodka, and gin can be referred to as **liquor**.

○ *Bars in the area can serve liquor up to 3:00am.*

○ *Room service can deliver liquor and nonalcoholic drinks.*

---

lob|by /lɒbi/ (lobbies)

GENERAL

NOUN In a hotel or other large building, the **lobby** is the area near the entrance that usually has corridors and staircases leading off it.

○ *In the hotel lobby you'll find an inviting sitting area next to reception.*

○ *Have a seat in the lobby and I'll fetch you when the cab arrives.*

lob|ster /lɒbstər/ (lobsters)

FOOD AND DRINK: FISH AND SEAFOOD

COUNT/NONCOUNT NOUN A **lobster** is a sea creature with a hard shell and two large claws. Its flesh is often eaten as food.

○ *Many seafood restaurants offer lobster and crab.*

○ *To serve cooked lobster, twist off the claws first.*

lock /lɒk/ (locks)

HOTEL ROOM: BEDROOM

NOUN The **lock** on something such as a door or a drawer is the device which is used to keep it shut and prevent other people from opening it. Locks are opened with a key.

○ *The lock to her room did not work.*

○ *I inserted the key in the lock of room number nine.*

low floor /loʊ flɔr/ (low floors)

HOTEL ROOM: BEDROOM

NOUN A **low floor** in a hotel is the first floor, or a level that is a short distance from the first floor.

○ *If you have difficulty climbing stairs, ask for a room on a low floor.*

○ *Some elderly guests don't like climbing stairs, so give them a low floor room.*

Mm

---

maid /meɪd/ (maids)

HOTEL PERSONNEL

NOUN A **maid** is a woman who works as a servant in a hotel.

- ○ *A maid brought breakfast at nine o'clock.*
- ○ *Maids clean your room each day of your stay.*

---

mai|tre d' /meɪtrə diː/ (maitre d's)

HOTEL PERSONNEL

NOUN At a restaurant, the **maitre d'** is the head waiter.

- ○ *The maitre d' assured them that they would be served quickly.*
- ○ *The waiters left and the maitre d' followed them.*

---

make a com|plaint /meɪk ə kəmpleɪnt/ (makes a complaint, made a complaint, making a complaint)

GENERAL

PHRASE If a guest **makes a complaint**, they express their dissatisfaction with something.

- ○ *Make a complaint if you are not satisfied with the service.*
- ○ *If you wish to make a complaint in writing, you should contact the hotel manager.*

make a pho|to|cop|y /meɪk ə foʊtəkɒpi/ (makes a photocopy, made a photocopy, making a photocopy)

HOTEL FACILITIES: BUSINESS CENTER

PHRASE If you **make a photocopy** of a document, you make a copy of it using a photocopier.

○ He made a photocopy of the customer's check.

○ You can print documents or make photocopies at the business center.

make the bed /meɪk ðə bɛd/ (makes the bed, made the bed, making the bed)

HOUSEKEEPING AND MAINTENANCE

PHRASE If you **make the bed**, you arrange the sheets and blankets on it so someone can sleep there.

○ The chambermaid made the bed with fresh sheets.

○ To make the bed, remove all pillows and blankets from the bed.

mat|tress /mætrɪs/ (mattresses)

HOTEL ROOM: BEDROOM

NOUN A **mattress** is the large, flat object which is put on a bed to make it comfortable to sleep on.

○ The mattress and pillows are too soft.

○ Many hotels now offer beds with firm mattresses.

▶ **COLLOCATIONS:**
hard mattress
soft mattress

meas|ure /mɛʒər/ (measures)

HOTEL BAR

NOUN A **measure of** a strong alcoholic drink such as brandy or whiskey is an amount of it in a glass. In bars, a **measure** is an official standard amount.

○ He poured another large measure of whiskey.

○ You must only sell alcoholic drinks in approved measures.

me|di|um /mˈidiəm/

FOOD AND DRINK: MEAT

ADJECTIVE Meat that is **medium** is cooked so that the inside is pink.

○ *How would you like your steak cooked? Medium?*

○ *A medium steak should have a band of pink color in the middle.*

me|di|um dry white wine /mˈidiəm draɪ waɪt waɪn/
(medium dry white wines)

FOOD AND DRINK: ALCOHOLIC DRINKS

COUNT/NONCOUNT NOUN **Medium dry white wine** is white wine that is not very sweet.

○ *This is a medium dry white wine with a light taste.*

○ *Dry and medium dry white wines go well with seafood.*

me|di|um rare /mˈidiəm rɛər/

FOOD AND DRINK: MEAT

ADJECTIVE Meat that is **medium rare** is cooked lightly so that the inside is still red but warm.

○ *He said he wanted his steak medium rare.*

○ *Grill the steak for three minutes on each side for medium rare.*

me|di|um well /mˈidiəm wɛl/

FOOD AND DRINK: COOKING

ADJECTIVE Meat that is **medium well** is cooked so that the inside is slightly pink.

○ *I'd like a hamburger, medium well, with cheese.*

○ *The meat was cooked exactly as they ordered it – medium well.*

m

meet|ing room /mitɪŋ rum/ (meeting rooms)

HOTEL BAR

NOUN A **meeting room** is a room in a hotel where a number of people can have a meeting.

○ *Our business center has 15 first floor meeting rooms.*

○ *The hotel has installed meeting rooms for its corporate guests, with Internet access and televisions.*

ROOMS IN A HOTEL

The following are other types of room that you find in a hotel:

baggage storage room
a room where people can leave their baggage in order to collect it later

ballroom
a very large room that is used for dancing

bar
a room where alcoholic drinks are served

business center
a room with facilities such as computers and a fax machine, that allows guests to work while they are staying at the hotel

conference room
a large room where a number of people can have a conference

fitness center or **gym**
a large room, usually containing special equipment, where people go to do physical exercise and get fit

function room
a large room where formal dinners or parties can be held

lobby
the area near the entrance of a hotel that usually has corridors and staircases leading off it

M

meet|ings and con|fer|ence man|ag|er /mi̱tɪŋz ənd kɒ̱nfərəns mæ̱nɪdʒər/ (**meetings and conference managers**)

HOTEL BAR

NOUN A **meetings and conference manager** at a hotel is responsible for organizing business meetings and conferences there.

○ A meetings and conference manager will be available to help during your event.

○ Our meetings and conference manager works with you to develop the details of your conference.

mel|on /me̱lən/ (**melons**)

FOOD AND DRINK: FRUIT

COUNT/NONCOUNT NOUN A **melon** is a large fruit which is sweet and juicy inside and has a hard green or yellow skin.

○ Starters include melon or a vegetable soup.

○ Try a light appetizer such as slices of juicy melon and ham.

▶ **COLLOCATION:**
slice of melon

men|u /me̱nyu/ (**menus**)

RESTAURANT: EQUIPMENT

NOUN In a restaurant or at a formal meal, the **menu** is a list of the meals and drinks that are available.

○ A waiter offered him the menu.

○ Have you found anything on the menu that you like?

mez|za|nine /me̱zənin/ (**mezzanines**)

RESERVATIONS AND CHECKING IN AND OUT

NOUN A **mezzanine** is a small floor which is built between two main floors of a building.

○ The dining room is on the mezzanine, up a short flight of steps.

○ There are ten meeting rooms located on the mezzanine level of the hotel.

m

milk /mɪlk/

FOOD AND DRINK: BREAKFAST

NOUN **Milk** is the white liquid produced by cows, goats, and some other animals, which people drink and use to make butter, cheese, and yogurt.

○ I like milk in my coffee.

○ If a customer asks for coffee, bring milk and sugar.

▶ COLLOCATIONS:
milk bottle
milk carton
pint of milk

min|er|al wa|ter /mɪnərəl wɔtər/ (mineral waters)

HOTEL BAR

COUNT/NONCOUNT NOUN **Mineral water** is water that comes out of the ground naturally and is considered healthy to drink.

○ On the table, there was a bottle of mineral water and an ice bucket.

○ Would you prefer sparkling or still mineral water?

min|i|bar /mɪnibɑr/ (minibars)

HOTEL ROOM: BEDROOM

NOUN In a hotel room, a **minibar** is a small fridge containing alcoholic drinks.

○ One of my duties is to check the minibar in each room and restock it.

○ The drinks from the minibar are more expensive than the ones served in the bar downstairs.

mir|ror /mɪrər/ (mirrors)

HOTEL ROOM: BATHROOM

NOUN A **mirror** is a flat piece of glass which reflects light, so that when you look at it you can see yourself reflected in it.

○ When a mirror is broken, the glass must be replaced.

○ To clean a bathroom mirror, use a sponge with hot water.

mix a drink /mɪks ə drɪŋk/ (mixes a drink, mixed a drink, mixing a drink)

HOTEL BAR

PHRASE If you **mix a drink**, you prepare it by mixing other drinks together.

○ He went to the bar and mixed a drink.

○ The bartender mixed a drink of whiskey and soda.

mix|er /mɪksər/ (mixers)

HOTEL BAR

NOUN A **mixer** is a nonalcoholic drink such as fruit juice or soda that you mix with strong alcohol such as gin.

○ Order ice and mixers from the waiters at the table.

○ She had a measure of spirits with a fruit juice mixer.

mod|i|fy a res|er|va|tion /mɒdɪfaɪ ə rɛzərveɪʃən/ (modifies a reservation, modified a reservation, modifying a reservation)

RESERVATIONS AND CHECKING IN AND OUT

PHRASE If you **modify a reservation**, you change a detail of a booking because someone who has booked a room has asked you to.

○ Reception will be able to modify the reservation to add more guests.

○ How do I cancel or modify a reservation?

mov|ies on de|mand /muviz ɒn dɪmænd/

HOTEL FACILITIES

PHRASE **Movies on demand** is a service that allows you to choose and watch a movie on your television.

○ All hotel rooms include a flat screen television and free movies on demand.

○ In-room entertainment includes television, movies on demand, and radio.

mus|sels /mˈʌsəlz/

FOOD AND DRINK: FISH AND SEAFOOD

NOUN **Mussels** are a kind of shellfish that you can eat from their shells.

○ Remove the mussels from their shells.

○ Lobster is expensive, but mussels and clams are more affordable.

M

Nn

nap|kin /næpkɪn/ (napkins)

RESTAURANT: EQUIPMENT

NOUN A **napkin** is a square of cloth or paper that you use when you are eating to protect your clothes, or to wipe your mouth or hands.

○ The waitress gave him a napkin to wipe his hands.

○ Make sure there is a box of paper napkins on each table.

non|al|co|hol|ic beer /nɒn ælkəhɒlɪk bɪər/ (nonalcoholic beers)

RESTAURANT: EQUIPMENT

COUNT/NONCOUNT NOUN **Nonalcoholic beer** is beer that does not contain any alcohol.

○ Nonalcoholic beer is available for guests who don't drink alcohol.

○ Can nonalcoholic beer be served to people under 21?

no-smok|ing room /noʊ smoʊkɪŋ rum/ (no-smoking rooms)

RESTAURANT: EQUIPMENT

NOUN A **no-smoking room** in a hotel is a room intended for people who do not want to smoke.

○ We found it odd that there was an ashtray in a no-smoking room.

○ If you do not smoke, book a no-smoking room.

no smok|ing sign /noʊ smoʊkɪŋ saɪn/ (no smoking signs)

RESTAURANT: EQUIPMENT

NOUN A **no smoking sign** in a place is a notice to say that smoking is forbidden in that place.

○ Smoking is allowed in areas that do not display a no smoking sign.

○ There are no smoking signs in all the no-smoking rooms.

no|tice /noʊtɪs/ (notices)

HOTEL ROOM: BEDROOM

NOUN A **notice** is a written announcement in a place where everyone can read it.

○ Hang the "Do Not Disturb" notice on your door.

○ There is a notice in each room showing the evacuation route.

no va|can|cies /noʊ veɪkənsiz/

RESERVATIONS AND CHECKING IN AND OUT

PHRASE **No vacancies** is used on a notice at a hotel or guest house when there are no rooms available to rent.

○ A few hotels had "no vacancies" notices in their windows.

○ We're sorry, there are no vacancies in the hotel at present.

N

Oo

---

oc|cu|pan|cy rate /ɒkyəpənsi reɪt/ (**occupancy rates**)

RESTAURANT: EQUIPMENT

NOUN The **occupancy rate** at a hotel is the number of available rooms that are occupied over a period of time.

○ Last year the hotel's occupancy rate was 66 percent.

○ The highest occupancy rate was 79% of rooms taken by customers.

---

ol|ive /ɒlɪv/ (**olives**)

FOOD AND DRINK: VEGETABLES

NOUN **Olives** are small green or black fruits with a bitter taste. Olives are often pressed to make olive oil.

○ They provide a bowl of black and green olives.

○ We serve green olives as an appetizer.

▶ **COLLOCATIONS:**
black olive
green olive
olive pit

---

ome|let (BRIT **omelette**) /ɒmlɪt/ (**omelets**)

FOOD AND DRINK: BREAKFAST

NOUN An **omelet** is a type of food made by beating eggs and cooking them in a flat frying pan.

○ Eggs can be made into an omelet with cheese.

○ The kitchen staff were busy breaking eggs and frying omelets.

on|ion /ˈʌnyən/ (onions)

FOOD AND DRINK: VEGETABLES

NOUN An **onion** is a round vegetable with a light brown skin. It has many white layers on its inside which have a strong, sharp smell and taste.

○ Finely chop the onion, and add it to the pan with the garlic.

○ Remove the outer layers of the onions before you chop them.

▶ **COLLOCATIONS:**
chop onion
fry onion
peel onion

on tap /ɒn tæp/

HOTEL BAR

PHRASE If drinks are **on tap**, they come from a tap rather than from a bottle.

○ What drinks have you got on tap?

○ Filtered water is always on tap here.

o|pen a bot|tle /ˈoʊpən ə bɒtᵊl/ (opens a bottle, opened a bottle, opening a bottle)

HOTEL BAR

PHRASE If you **open a bottle**, you remove the cork or cap.

○ The barman opened the bottle of water.

○ How can you open a bottle of wine without a corkscrew?

op|tion|al /ˈɒpʃənᵊl/

RESTAURANT: PAYING THE CHECK

ADJECTIVE If something is **optional**, you can choose whether or not you do it or have it.

○ An optional service charge was added to the check.

○ If you did not think the service was good, do not pay the optional service charge.

▶ **COLLOCATION:**
optional extra

---

or|ange /ɔrɪndʒ/ (oranges)

FOOD AND DRINK: FRUIT

NOUN An **orange** is a round juicy fruit with a thick, orange-colored skin.

○ I squeezed the juice out of some oranges.

○ Orange and apple juices are available at breakfast.

▶ **COLLOCATION:**
orange juice

---

or|der¹ /ɔrdər/ (orders)

FOOD AND DRINK: DINING

NOUN Someone's **order** is what they have asked to be brought or made for them.

○ A waiter took their drink orders.

○ The waiter returned with her order and the customer signed the check.

▶ **COLLOCATIONS:**
place an order
take an order

---

or|der² /ɔrdər/ (orders, ordered, ordering)

FOOD AND DRINK: DINING

TRANSITIVE/INTRANSITIVE VERB When you **order** something, such as food, you ask for it to be brought to you or made for you.

○ They ordered coffee before they asked for the check.

○ I ordered chicken, but the waitress brought fish.

or|der a drink /ɔrdər ə drɪŋk/ (orders a drink, ordered a drink, ordering a drink)

HOTEL BAR

PHRASE When a customer **orders a drink**, they ask for it to be brought to them.

○ He stopped at the bar to order a drink and a sandwich.

○ He returned to the hotel and ordered a drink from the bartender.

or|der room ser|vice /ɔrdər rum sɜrvɪs/ (orders room service, ordered room service, ordering room service)

GENERAL

PHRASE When a customer **orders room service**, they ask for meals or drinks to be brought to their room.

○ She dined in the hotel's dining room instead of ordering room service.

○ Whenever you order room service, you are asked to repeat your order.

out|let /aʊtlɪt/ (outlets)

HOTEL ROOM: BEDROOM

NOUN An **outlet** is a place, usually in a wall, where you can connect electrical devices to the electricity supply.

○ Their room had two electrical outlets for shavers.

○ Plug the hairdryer into any electric outlet.

▶ SYNONYMS:
plug
socket

o|ver eas|y /oʊvər izi/

FOOD AND DRINK: BREAKFAST

PHRASE If a fried egg is served **over easy**, it is cooked on both sides.

○ We would like a couple of eggs over easy, bacon, and coffee.

○ He ordered one egg sunny side up and one egg over easy.

oys|ter /ɔɪstər/ (oysters)

FOOD AND DRINK: FISH AND SEAFOOD

NOUN An **oyster** is a large flat shellfish.

○ The restaurant specializes in oysters and other shellfish.

○ Oysters and mussels are served in their shells.

Pp

pack|age /pækɪdʒ/ (packages)

RESERVATIONS AND CHECKING IN AND OUT

NOUN A **package** is a set of services and features that are included in the cost of a stay in a hotel.

○ *The hotel did not charge extra for the food, counting it as one of the guest meals included in the package.*

○ *Our business package includes Internet access and car parking.*

pan|cake /pænkeɪk/ (pancakes)

FOOD AND DRINK: BREAKFAST

NOUN A **pancake** is a thin, flat, circular piece of cooked batter made from milk, flour, and eggs. Pancakes are usually eaten for breakfast, with butter and syrup.

○ *The restaurant serves omelets, pancakes, and waffles at breakfast.*

○ *She ordered a stack of pancakes with butter.*

pants press (in BRIT use **trouser press**) /pænts prɛs/ (pants presses)

HOTEL ROOM: BEDROOM

NOUN A **pants press** in a hotel room is a machine that you put a pair of pants inside to get rid of the creases.

○ *Use the pants press to keep your pants smart.*

○ *If there's a pants press in the room, use it to smooth the wrinkles out of pant legs.*

park|ing gar|age /pɑrkɪŋ gərɑʒ/ (parking garages)

HOTEL FACILITIES

NOUN A **parking garage** is a building where people can leave their cars.

○ We have good parking facilities in our parking garage for guests.

○ If our parking garage is full, you can park in the lot nearby.

park|ing lot (in BRIT use car park) /pɑrkɪŋ lɒt/ (parking lots)

HOTEL FACILITIES

NOUN A **parking lot** is an area of ground where people can leave their cars.

○ The hotel provides a private parking lot for up to 30 cars.

○ The parking lot is located beneath the hotel building.

par|ty /pɑrti/ (parties)

RESTAURANT: DINING

NOUN A **party of** people is a group of people who are doing something together, for example, eating at a restaurant or staying in a hotel.

○ Can you seat a party of four for dinner?

○ Has the Smith party checked in yet?

P

pâ|té /pɑtei/

FOOD AND DRINK: MEAT

NOUN **Pâté** is a soft mixture of meat, fish, or vegetables with various flavorings that is eaten cold.

○ Chicken liver pâté is served with toast.

○ A pâté made with salmon is a delicious appetizer.

pay /peɪ/ (pays, paid, paying)

FOOD AND DRINK: DINING

VERB When you **pay** something such as a check or a debt, you pay the amount that you owe.

○ I'd like to pay by check.

○ I must ask you to pay for your meal before you leave.

▶ COLLOCATIONS:
   pay a fee
   pay cash

---

pay the check (in BRIT use **pay the bill**) /peɪ ðə tʃɛk/ (**pays the check, paid the check, paying the check**)

RESTAURANT: PAYING THE CHECK

PHRASE When a customer **pays the check** in a restaurant, they pay the amount that they owe for their meal.

○ He finished his coffee and paid the check with cash.

○ They canceled the rest of their meal and paid the check.

---

pay T|V /peɪ ti vi/

HOTEL ROOM: BEDROOM

NOUN **Pay TV** is television that you can watch only if you pay a fee such as a subscription to a satellite or cable television company.

○ Pay TV is free of charge to guests, offering a wide choice of channels.

○ Hotel rooms include television with pay TV and radio.

---

pho|to|cop|i|er /foʊtəkɒpiər/ (**photocopiers**)

HOTEL FACILITIES: BUSINESS CENTER

NOUN A **photocopier** is a machine that quickly copies documents onto paper by photographing them.

○ The hotel has a business center with a computer, printer, and photocopier.

○ If you need to make copies of an important document, the hotel has a photocopier that is available for guests.

pho|to|cop|y /fóʊtəkɒpi/ (photocopies, photocopied, photocopying)

HOTEL FACILITIES: BUSINESS CENTER

VERB If you **photocopy** a document, you make a copy of it using a photocopier.

○ Contact reception if you need to photocopy documents.

○ Photocopy the receipt and give the original to the guest.

pil|low /pɪloʊ/ (pillows)

HOTEL ROOM: BEDROOM

NOUN A **pillow** is a rectangular cushion that you rest your head on when you are in bed.

○ Ask reception if you need more pillows for the bed.

○ She took extra pillows and comforters from the shelves for the beds.

pil|low|case /pɪloʊkeɪs/ (pillowcases)

HOTEL ROOM: BEDROOM

NOUN A **pillowcase** is a cover for a pillow that can be removed and washed.

○ Remove and wash used pillowcases.

○ One of the pillows on the bed has a different pillowcase from the others.

pitch|er /pɪtʃər/ (pitchers)

RESTAURANT: EQUIPMENT

NOUN A **pitcher** is a cylindrical container with a handle and is used for holding and pouring liquids.

○ The waiter fetched a pitcher of iced water.

○ Pour orange juice and pineapple juice in a large pitcher and add mineral water.

plate | 104

plate /pleɪt/ (plates)

RESTAURANT: EQUIPMENT

NOUN A **plate** is a round or oval flat dish that is used to hold food.

○ *A waiter came to clear our plates and refill glasses.*

○ *Give me a plate of ham and eggs for breakfast.*

> **RELATED WORDS**
>
> The following are types of plate with a particular purpose:
>
> **bread plate**
> a small plate for bread that you eat along with your main meal
>
> **dinner plate**
> a plate on which a large meal is served

---

please clean my room sign /pliz klin maɪ rum saɪn/ (please clean my room signs)

HOTEL ROOM: BEDROOM

NOUN A **please clean my room sign** is a sign that a guest in a hotel hangs outside their room to tell the cleaner the room is available for cleaning.

○ *Hang a please clean my room sign on the door when you go out.*

○ *The maid will clean your room if the please clean my room sign is on the door handle.*

---

plug¹ /plʌg/ (plugs)

HOTEL ROOM: BATHROOM

NOUN A **plug** on a piece of electrical equipment is a small plastic object with two or three metal pins that fit into the holes of an electric outlet, allowing the equipment to connect to the electricity supply.

○ *The lamp needed a new plug.*

○ *I replaced the fuse in the plug.*

plug² /plʌg/ (plugs)

HOTEL ROOM: BATHROOM

NOUN A **plug** is a thick, circular piece of rubber or plastic that you use to block the hole in a bathtub or sink when it is filled with water.

○ She put the plug in the basin and filled it with cold water.

○ I want to take a bath, but the bathtub plug is missing.

poached egg /poutʃt ɛg/ (poached eggs)

HOTEL ROOM: BATHROOM

NOUN A **poached egg** has been cooked gently in boiling water without its shell.

○ He had a light breakfast of poached eggs and tea.

○ Would you like poached eggs or boiled eggs with your toast?

pol|ish¹ /pɒlɪʃ/

HOUSEKEEPING AND MAINTENANCE

NOUN **Polish** is a substance that you put on the surface of an object in order to clean it, protect it, and make it shine.

○ Use polish to clean the counter.

○ The polish makes the floor shiny.

pol|ish² /pɒlɪʃ/ (polishes, polished, polishing)

HOUSEKEEPING AND MAINTENANCE

VERB If you **polish** something, you put polish on it or rub it with a cloth to make it shine.

○ Once a week she polished the floor in the entrance hall.

○ To add shine to furniture, polish it with a cloth.

P

pork /pɔrk/

FOOD AND DRINK: MEAT

NOUN **Pork** is meat from a pig, usually fresh and not smoked or salted.

○ *She ordered roasted pork loin with potato purée and carrots.*

○ *Make sure the pork chops are cooked all the way through.*

▶ COLLOCATION:
pork chop

---

por|ter /pɔrtər/ (**porters**)

HOTEL PERSONNEL

NOUN A **porter** is a person whose job is to carry things, for example, people's luggage at a hotel.

○ *The taxi pulled up at the hotel and a porter sprinted to the door.*

○ *Our porter will carry your bags upstairs.*

---

po|ta|to /pəteɪtoʊ/ (**potatoes**)

FOOD AND DRINK: VEGETABLES

COUNT/NONCOUNT NOUN **Potatoes** are round vegetables with brown or red skins and white insides.

○ *Roast meats are usually served with potatoes and vegetables.*

○ *Potatoes can be roasted, boiled, or baked.*

▶ COLLOCATIONS:
baked potato
boiled potato
fried potato
mashed potato
roast potato

P

poul|try /poʊltri/

FOOD AND DRINK: MEAT

PLURAL/NONCOUNT NOUN You can refer to chickens, ducks, and other birds that are kept for their eggs and meat as **poultry**.

○ The menu features roast chicken, duck, and other poultry.

○ Poultry and game birds must be cooked thoroughly.

pour¹ /pɔr/ (pours, poured, pouring)

FOOD AND DRINK: COOKING

VERB If you **pour** a liquid or other substance, you make it flow steadily out of a container by holding the container at an angle.

○ Pour sauce on two plates and arrange the meat neatly.

○ The server poured juice into a glass.

pour² /pɔr/ (pours, poured, pouring)

FOOD AND DRINK: COOKING

VERB If you **pour** someone a drink, you put some of the drink in a cup or glass so that they can drink it.

○ He poured the customer another drink.

○ The bartender poured her a glass of water.

P

prawn /prɔn/ (prawns)

FOOD AND DRINK: FISH AND SEAFOOD

NOUN A **prawn** is a small shellfish with a long tail and many legs, which can be eaten.

○ Peel the prawns, leaving the tails on.

○ Our prawns and shrimp are freshly caught each day.

print /prɪnt/ (**prints, printed, printing**)

RESTAURANT: PAYING THE CHECK

VERB If you **print** words, you write in letters that are not joined together.

○ *Print and sign your name there please.*

○ *Please print your details clearly, using block capitals.*

---

print|er /prɪntər/ (**printers**)

HOTEL FACILITIES: BUSINESS CENTER

NOUN A **printer** is a machine that can be connected to a computer in order to make copies on paper of documents or other information held by the computer.

○ *The assistant printed the document on the printer in reception.*

○ *In the business center there are printers connected to PCs.*

▶ **COLLOCATIONS:**
ink-jet printer
laser printer

---

pri|or|i|ty check-in /praɪɔrɪti tʃɛk ɪn/ (**priority check-ins**)

HOTEL FACILITIES: BUSINESS CENTER

COUNT/NONCOUNT NOUN **Priority check-in** at a hotel is an arrangement which allows a guest to check in without waiting in a line.

○ *Priority check-in and late check-out can be arranged for a small extra charge.*

○ *Check in at our designated priority check-in desk for only $15.*

pri|or|i|ty guest /praɪɔ̠rɪti gɛst/ (**priority guests**)

HOTEL FACILITIES: BUSINESS CENTER

NOUN A **priority guest** at a hotel is a regular guest who has special rights, such as early check-in and discounts on food.

○ The hotel offers priority guest services for customers who have joined its loyalty program.

○ There are also non-smoking rooms and priority guest rooms.

---

prix fixe /pri̠ fi̠ks/ (**prix fixes**)

FOOD AND DRINK: DINING

NOUN In a restaurant, a **prix fixe** is a menu with a specific set of meals to choose from. The price charged for each meal is the same and does not vary.

○ Ask for the set meal or prix fixe in a restaurant.

○ Our chefs are now offering a prix fixe dinner menu to help guests save money.

> **PRONUNCIATION**
>
> Note the silent "x" in the word "prix."

P

---

pud|ding /pʊ̠dɪŋ/ (**puddings**)

FOOD AND DRINK: DINING

COUNT/NONCOUNT NOUN A **pudding** is a cooked sweet food made from ingredients such as milk, sugar, flour, and eggs, and is served either hot or cold.

○ The desserts included a baked apple pudding.

○ Have a hot banana pudding after your main meal.

Qq

queen-sized bed /kwin saɪzd bɛd/ (**queen-sized beds**)

HOTEL FACILITIES: BUSINESS CENTER

NOUN A **queen-sized bed** is larger than a double bed, but smaller than a king-sized bed.

○ *The queen-sized beds are fitted with linen sheets.*

○ *The luxury double room has a queen-sized bed.*

Rr

rack rate /ræk reɪt/ (rack rates)

HOTEL FACILITIES: BUSINESS CENTER

NOUN The **rack rate** is the normal price of a hotel room, before any discount.

○ A second room can be reserved at a 50 percent discount off the rack rate.

○ Rack rates for a hotel room start at $220 a night.

> **RELATED WORDS**
>
> Compare **rack rate** with **corporate rate**, which is the price charged to a guest who is staying at a hotel while traveling for business, and **walk-up rate**, which is the price charged to a guest who arrives without a reservation.

ra|di|o /reɪdioʊ/ (radios)

HOTEL ROOM: BEDROOM

NOUN A **radio** is the piece of equipment that you use in order to listen to radio programs.

○ They had a television and radio in the room.

○ All the rooms have a satellite television and digital radio.

rare /rɛər/

FOOD AND DRINK: MEAT

ADJECTIVE Meat that is **rare** is cooked very lightly so that the inside is still red and cold.

r

○ Thick tuna steaks are eaten rare, like beef.

○ Some customers want rare steaks with a cool center.

RELATED WORDS

The following are also terms that relate to how well cooked a piece of meat is:

medium rare
cooked lightly so that the inside is still red but warm

medium
cooked so that the inside is pink

medium well
cooked so that the inside is slightly pink

well done
cooked thoroughly

---

ra|zor /ˈreɪzər/ (razors)

HOTEL ROOM: BATHROOM

NOUN A **razor** is a tool that people use for shaving.

○ The hotel offered toothbrushes, razors, and other bathroom items to guests who forgot them.

○ If you need to shave, reception will give you a disposable razor.

---

re|ceipt /rɪˈsiːt/ (receipts)

RESTAURANT: PAYING THE CHECK

NOUN A **receipt** is a piece of paper that you get from someone as proof that they have received money or goods from you.

○ After you've paid for your meal we will give you a receipt.

○ I wrote her a receipt for the money she paid.

PRONUNCIATION

Note the silent "p" in this word.

re|cep|tion /rɪsɛpʃ°n/

GENERAL

NOUN **Reception** in a hotel is the desk or office that books rooms for people and answers their questions.

○ I went down to the hotel reception at 7:45 and checked out.

○ Please hand in your room key at the reception desk when you leave.

▶ **COLLOCATIONS:**
  reception desk
  reception staff

re|cep|tion|ist /rɪsɛpʃənɪst/ (receptionists)

HOTEL PERSONNEL

NOUN In a hotel, the **receptionist** is the person whose job is to reserve rooms for people and answer their questions.

○ The receptionist greeted him before asking his name.

○ The receptionist will check you in and give you a key card.

red wine /rɛd waɪn/ (red wines)

FOOD AND DRINK: ALCOHOLIC DRINKS

COUNT/NONCOUNT NOUN **Red wine** is wine that is dark red in color.

○ Red wine goes well with meat and white wine goes well with fish.

○ Some customers prefer red wine to white wine.

ref|use a card /rɪfyuz ə kɑrd/ (refuses a card, refused a card, refusing a card)

RESERVATIONS AND CHECKING IN AND OUT

PHRASE If you **refuse a card**, you do not allow someone's credit card to be used to pay a bill.

○ Refuse a credit card that is not signed.

○ I refused his card as payment because it was damaged.

r

re|mote con|trol /rɪmoʊt kəntroʊl/ (**remote controls**)

HOTEL ROOM: BEDROOM

NOUN The **remote control** for a television or other equipment is the device that you use to control the machine from a distance, by pressing the buttons on it.

○ *The remote control for the television is missing from the room.*

○ *Check the remote control operates the television in each room.*

re|pair /rɪpɛər/ (**repairs, repaired, repairing**)

GENERAL

VERB If you **repair** something that has been damaged or is not working properly, you fix it.

○ *The staff came promptly to repair the broken lock on the room door.*

○ *If the television does not work, we will send someone to repair it.*

▶ **COLLOCATION:**
repair the damage

re|place /rɪpleɪs/ (**replaces, replaced, replacing**)

HOUSEKEEPING AND MAINTENANCE

VERB If you **replace** something that is used, damaged, or lost, you get a new one to use instead.

○ *The shower has broken and we have to replace it.*

○ *Replace any bottles taken from the minibar.*

re|plen|ish /rɪplɛnɪʃ/ (**replenishes, replenished, replenishing**)

HOUSEKEEPING AND MAINTENANCE

VERB If you **replenish** something, you make it full or complete again.

○ *Check and replenish the minibar in the rooms every day.*

○ *The chambermaids replenish any toiletries that guests have used.*

res|er|va|tion /rɛzərveɪʃᵊn/ (reservations)

RESERVATIONS AND CHECKING IN AND OUT

NOUN If you make a **reservation**, you arrange for something such as a table in a restaurant or a room in a hotel to be kept for you.

○ He went to the desk to inquire and make a reservation.

○ How many people do you want to make a reservation for?

res|er|va|tions man|ag|er /rɛzərveɪʃᵊnz mænɪdʒər/ (reservations managers)

GENERAL

NOUN A **reservations manager** at a hotel is responsible for the reservations at the hotel.

○ If you have questions about reservations, call the reservations manager.

○ The reservations manager offered them a room at a discount.

re|serve a room /rɪzɜrv ə rum/ (reserves a room, reserved a room, reserving a room)

RESERVATIONS AND CHECKING IN AND OUT

PHRASE If you **reserve a room** at a hotel, you keep it for a person who is going to arrive on an agreed date.

○ I have reserved a room for you in the hotel.

○ Reserve two rooms under the guest's name.

re|spond to a com|plaint /rɪspɒnd tu ə kəmpleɪnt/ (responds to a complaint, responded to a complaint, responding to a complaint)

RESERVATIONS AND CHECKING IN AND OUT

PHRASE If you **respond to a complaint**, you answer a customer who expressed their dissatisfaction with something.

○ How quickly do you want us to respond to a complaint if we have one?

○ The guest relations manager is responsible for responding to complaints from customers.

res|tau|rant /rɛstərɑnt/ (restaurants)

GENERAL

NOUN A **restaurant** is a place where you can eat a meal and pay for it. In restaurants, your food is usually served to you at your table by a waiter or waitress.

○ The restaurant serves breakfast, lunch, and dinner.

○ The food at the restaurant was good and the waiters were polite.

re|stock /ristɒk/ (restocks, restocked, restocking)

HOUSEKEEPING AND MAINTENANCE

VERB If you **restock** something such as a minibar or bathroom shelf, you fill it with food or other goods to replace what you have used.

○ Housekeeping replaced the towels and restocked the toiletries in the bathroom.

○ Staff will check and restock the minibar when they clean the room.

re|verse a charge /rivɜrs ə tʃɑrdʒ/ (reverses a charge, reversed a charge, reversing a charge)

RESERVATIONS AND CHECKING IN AND OUT

PHRASE If you **reverse a charge** on a credit card, you put the amount you have charged back into the credit card account.

○ The credit card was charged twice. I need to reverse a charge.

○ The hotel did not reverse the charge when he canceled his reservation.

R

re|volv|ing door /rivɒlvɪŋ dɔr/ (revolving doors)

GENERAL

NOUN Some large buildings have **revolving doors** instead of an ordinary door. They consist of four glass doors which turn together in a circle around a vertical post.

○ When you arrive, go through the revolving doors that lead into the lobby.

○ The hotel lobby is entered through tall glass revolving doors.

roll /rɔʊl/ (rolls)

FOOD AND DRINK: BREAKFAST

NOUN A **roll** is a small piece of bread that is round or long and is made to be eaten by one person. Rolls can be eaten plain, with butter, or with a filling.

○ *The waitress came in with bread rolls and coffee.*

○ *He sipped at his coffee and spread butter on a roll.*

room key /rum ki/ (room keys)

FOOD AND DRINK: BREAKFAST

NOUN A **room key** is a key given to a guest in a hotel in order to open or lock the door of their room.

○ *When you leave your room in the morning, leave your room key in the lock.*

○ *The receptionist will give you a room key when you check in.*

room oc|cu|pan|cy tax (ABBR ROT) /rum ɒkyəpənsi tæks/

GENERAL

NOUN **Room occupancy tax** is a tax that guests at a hotel have to pay in order to stay there.

○ *The 6 percent room occupancy tax applies to any room in the hotel.*

○ *There is a 14% sales tax plus a $2 per night room occupancy tax.*

room on|ly /rum ounli/

RESERVATIONS AND CHECKING IN AND OUT

PHRASE **Room only** is used to indicate that the price of accommodations in a hotel or guest house does not include the cost of food.

○ *A two-night stay for two (room only) costs $100. Dinner costs from $20.*

○ *He booked a stay on a room only basis for seven nights.*

room ser|vice /rum sɜrvɪs/

GENERAL

NOUN **Room service** is a service in a hotel by which meals or drinks are provided for guests in their rooms.

○ Guests can place an order for room service on the phone by dialing 118.

○ Dine in the hotel restaurant or order food from room service.

root beer /rut bɪər/ (root beers)

HOTEL BAR

COUNT/NONCOUNT NOUN **Root beer** is a carbonated nonalcoholic drink flavored with the roots of various plants and herbs.

○ They offer root beer and other nonalcoholic drinks.

○ The herbs in root beer give it a characteristic flavor.

ro|sé wine /rouzeɪ waɪn/ (rosé wines)

HOTEL BAR

COUNT/NONCOUNT NOUN **Rosé wine** is wine that is pink in color.

○ White and rosé wines should be served chilled for about 1–2 hours in a refrigerator.

○ The majority of wines served in this restaurant are red wines or rosé wines.

R

round up /raʊnd ʌp/ (rounds up, rounded up, rounding up)

RESTAURANT: PAYING THE CHECK

VERB If you **round** an amount **up**, you change it to the nearest whole number or nearest multiple of 10, 100, 1000, and so on.

○ Round up the total price to the nearest dollar.

○ At restaurants you should round up the bill or tip up to 10%.

rug /rʌg/ (rugs)

HOTEL ROOM: BEDROOM

NOUN A **rug** is a piece of thick material that you put on a floor. It is like a carpet but covers a smaller area.

○ There were woolen rugs on the floorboards.

○ Straighten all the rugs or people might trip over them.

Ss

safe /seɪf/ (safes)

HOTEL ROOM: BEDROOM

NOUN A **safe** is a strong metal cabinet with special locks, in which you keep money, jewelry, or other valuable things.

- ○ *Always put your passport in the hotel safe.*
- ○ *The reception is open 24 hours and there is a safe available for guests' valuables.*

safe de|pos|it box /seɪf dɪpɒzɪt bɒks/ (safe deposit boxes)

HOTEL FACILITIES

NOUN A **safe deposit box** is a small box, kept by the hotel in a secure place, in which you can store valuable objects.

- ○ *Guests will find safe deposit boxes in the reception area where valuables can be kept.*
- ○ *Your items are stored in a safe deposit box behind the front desk.*

sa|la|mi /səlɑ̱mi/

FOOD AND DRINK: MEAT

NOUN **Salami** is a type of strong-flavored sausage. It is usually thinly sliced and eaten cold.

- ○ *She arranged the slices of ham, salami, chicken, and other meats on a serving dish.*
- ○ *The cold meat and sausage platter includes beef and salami.*

sales man|ag|er /seɪlz mænɪdʒər/ (**sales managers**)

HOTEL FACILITIES

NOUN A **sales manager** is responsible for selling the accommodations at a hotel.

○ The goal of a sales manager is to find new ways to increase sales.

○ The hotel sales manager often visits potential customers.

---

sales tax /seɪlz tæks/

RESERVATIONS AND CHECKING IN AND OUT

NOUN The **sales tax** on food or accommodations is the percentage of money that you pay to the local or state government.

○ A 6% sales tax on complimentary hotel rooms began this month.

○ A restaurant must charge a sales tax on the meals it sells.

---

salm|on /sæmən/

FOOD AND DRINK: FISH AND SEAFOOD

NOUN **Salmon** is the orangey-pink flesh of a large silver-colored fish which is eaten as food. It is often smoked and eaten raw.

○ The fish course is smoked salmon served on salad.

○ The wedding party enjoyed a luxurious appetizer of smoked salmon with champagne.

▶ COLLOCATION:
smoked salmon

S

---

salt /sɔlt/

FOOD AND DRINK: HERBS AND SPICES

NOUN **Salt** is a strong-tasting substance, in the form of white powder or crystals, which is used to improve the flavor of food or to preserve it. Salt occurs naturally in sea water.

○ Season the food lightly with salt and pepper.

○ Put pots of salt and pepper on the tables.

sauce /sɔs/ (sauces)

FOOD AND DRINK: MEAT

COUNT/NONCOUNT NOUN A **sauce** is a thick liquid which is served with other food.

○ The pasta is cooked in a sauce of garlic, tomatoes, and cheese.

○ Pour the mushroom sauce over the steaks and serve them.

sau|sage /sɔsɪdʒ/ (sausages)

FOOD AND DRINK: BREAKFAST

NOUN A **sausage** consists of minced meat, usually pork, mixed with other ingredients and is contained in a tube made of skin or a similar material.

○ The restaurant turns out delicious homemade treats such as pork sausages.

○ We serve different types of sausage, including salami and pepperoni.

scram|bled eggs /skræmbᵊld ɛgz/

FOOD AND DRINK: BREAKFAST

NOUN **Scrambled eggs** are eggs that are mixed together and then cooked in butter.

○ I prefer scrambled eggs to poached eggs.

○ Do you want boiled eggs or scrambled eggs with breakfast?

sea|food /sifud/

FOOD AND DRINK: FISH AND SEAFOOD

NOUN **Seafood** is shellfish such as lobsters, mussels, and crabs, and sometimes other sea creatures that you can eat.

○ The restaurant serves plates of seafood including mussels, crabs, and calamari.

○ Seafood restaurants specialize in fish and shellfish.

S

sea salt /siː sɔlt/

FOOD AND DRINK: HERBS AND SPICES

NOUN **Sea salt** is salt that you obtain by evaporating sea water.

○ Season the fish with sea salt and black pepper.

○ Sea salt has a stronger taste than regular salt.

se|cond sit|ting /sɛkənd sɪtɪŋ/ (**second sittings**)

HOTEL PERSONNEL

NOUN A **second sitting** is the second period when a meal is served if there is not enough space for everyone to eat at the same time.

○ First sitting is best if you're hungry, but second sitting is more relaxed.

○ The second sitting in the restaurant is at 8:30 (the first is at 6:30).

se|cu|ri|ty guard /sɪkyʊərɪti gɑrd/ (**security guards**)

HOTEL PERSONNEL

NOUN A **security guard** is someone whose job is to protect a building.

○ Security guards watch over the hotel grounds.

○ The man was stopped at the door by a security guard.

see the men|u /si ðə mɛnyu/ (**sees the menu, saw the menu, seen the menu, seeing the menu**)

FOOD AND DRINK: DINING

PHRASE When a customer asks to **see the menu**, they ask you to bring them a copy of the menu.

○ She ordered drinks and asked to see the menu.

○ The waiter will ask you if you want to see the menu.

S

send a fax /sɛnd ə fæks/ (**sends a fax, sent a fax, sending a fax**)

HOTEL FACILITIES: BUSINESS CENTER

PHRASE If you **send a fax**, you send a copy of a document from one fax machine to another.

○ *Can I receive and send a fax at the hotel?*

○ *A business center is available, where you can make a photocopy or send a fax.*

---

serve /sɜrv/ (serves, served, serving)

FOOD AND DRINK: COOKING

VERB When you **serve** food and drinks, you give people food and drinks.

○ *Food is not served in the evenings until six o'clock.*

○ *Serve soup with bread or crackers.*

---

ser|vice a room /sɜrvɪs ə rum/ (services a room, serviced a room, servicing a room)

GENERAL

PHRASE If you **service a room**, you clean it and change the towels and bed linen in it.

○ *Housekeeping are still cleaning and servicing the rooms at the moment.*

○ *We had to service our own rooms and stock our own minibar.*

---

ser|vice charge /sɜrvɪs tʃɑrdʒ/ (service charges)

RESTAURANT: PAYING THE CHECK

NOUN A **service charge** is an amount that is added to your bill in a restaurant to pay for the work of the person who comes and serves you.

○ *Most restaurants add a 10 percent service charge to the check.*

○ *There's a 15% service charge which is added to the total bill.*

---

set men|u /sɛt mɛnyu/ (set menus)

FOOD AND DRINK: DINING

NOUN A **set menu** is a menu with a specific set of meals to choose from. The price charged for each meal is the same.

○ *There is a single set menu, with four courses for $31.*

○ *Our set menu is offered alongside the à la carte menu.*

sew|ing kit /soʊɪŋ kɪt/ (**sewing kits**)

FOOD AND DRINK: DINING

NOUN A **sewing kit** is a small package containing items, such as needles and thread, that you need to sew something.

○ Needles and thread are included in the sewing kit.

○ There was no sewing kit in the room to mend my shirt.

sham|poo /ʃæmpu/

HOTEL ROOM: BATHROOM

NOUN **Shampoo** is a soapy liquid that you use for washing your hair.

○ Does the hotel supply toiletries such as shampoo and soap?

○ There is a small bottle of shampoo on the bathroom shelf.

▶ **COLLOCATION:**
 bottle of shampoo

shav|ing mir|ror /ʃeɪvɪŋ mɪrər/ (**shaving mirrors**)

FOOD AND DRINK: DINING

NOUN A **shaving mirror** is a small, often round, mirror that can be moved out from a wall, and which you use to see your reflection when you are shaving your face.

○ The shaving mirror is next to the basin and is mounted on a retractable arm.

○ There is no shaving mirror so it is difficult to shave.

sheet /ʃit/ (**sheets**)

HOTEL ROOM: BEDROOM

NOUN A **sheet** is a large rectangular piece of cotton or other cloth that you sleep on or cover yourself with in a bed.

○ Once a week, a maid changes the sheets on the bed.

○ The room has comfortable bedding and clean sheets.

▶ **COLLOCATIONS:**
 change the sheets
 cotton sheet

shell|fish /ʃɛlfɪʃ/

FOOD AND DRINK: FISH AND SEAFOOD

NOUN **Shellfish** are small creatures that live in the sea and have a shell. Some types of shellfish are eaten as food.

○ *Shellfish such as mussels and clams are the specialties in this restaurant.*

○ *Remove the shellfish from their shells and add them to the pan.*

shot /ʃɒt/ (shots)

HOTEL BAR

NOUN A **shot** of a strong alcoholic drink is a small glass of it.

○ *Pour a shot of vodka into a glass.*

○ *The men were drinking shots at the bar.*

shot glass /ʃɒt glæs/ (shot glasses)

HOTEL BAR

NOUN A **shot glass** is a small glass without a stem which you use for drinking shots.

○ *He poured the drinks in small shot glasses.*

○ *The waiter placed a shot glass containing a measure of whiskey on the table.*

show|er /ʃaʊər/ (showers)

HOTEL ROOM: BATHROOM

NOUN A **shower** is a device for washing yourself. It consists of a pipe which ends in a flat cover with a lot of holes in it so that water comes out in a spray. It is often contained in a small enclosed area.

○ *Some rooms have showers rather than bathtubs.*

○ *There is no hot water in the shower.*

▶ **COLLOCATION:**
take a shower

show to a ta|ble /ʃoʊ tu ə teɪbəl/ (**shows to a table, showed to a table, shown to a table, showing to a table**)

RESTAURANT

PHRASE When you **show** a customer **to a table** in a restaurant, you take them to the table where you want them to sit and help them sit down.

○ *A waitress showed them to a table and took their order.*

○ *Good evening, let me show you to your table.*

side dish /saɪd dɪʃ/ (**side dishes**)

RESTAURANT

NOUN A **side dish** is a portion of food served at the same time as the main dish.

○ *These mushrooms make a delicious side dish.*

○ *Serve roasted vegetables as a side dish with roast chicken.*

sign a check (in BRIT use **sign a bill**) /saɪn ə tʃɛk/ (**signs a check, signed a check, signing a check**)

RESTAURANT: PAYING THE CHECK

PHRASE When you **sign a check**, you write your name on it in a special space in order to validate it.

○ *The guest signed the check and left.*

○ *Excuse me Madam, you forgot to sign this check.*

sig|na|ture /sɪgnətʃər/ (**signatures**)

RESTAURANT: PAYING THE CHECK

NOUN Your **signature** is your name, written in your own characteristic way, often at the end of a document to indicate that you wrote the document or that you agree with what it says.

○ *I wrote my signature at the bottom of the page.*

○ *Please print your name and write your signature on the booking form.*

S

sil|ver|ware (in BRIT use **cutlery**) /sɪlvərwɛər/

RESTAURANT: EQUIPMENT

NOUN You can use **silverware** to refer to all the things in a restaurant that are made of silver, especially the flatware and dishes.

○ She cleaned the knife and put it on the table with the rest of the silverware.

○ There was a spoon missing when I put the silverware back.

sin|gle room /sɪŋɡəl rum/ (**single rooms**)

HOTEL ROOM: BEDROOM

NOUN A **single room** is a room intended for one person to stay in.

○ Choose from twin or single rooms, all of which are comfortable.

○ Each guest has her own single room, or shares a double room.

> **RELATED WORDS**
>
> Compare **single room** with **double room**, which is a room intended for two people, usually a couple, to stay in.

slip|pers /slɪpərz/

HOTEL ROOM: BEDROOM

NOUN **Slippers** are loose, soft shoes that you wear in your room.

○ Bathrooms include bathrobes and slippers.

○ To make you even more comfortable we give you slippers and a bathrobe.

▶ **COLLOCATIONS:**
bedroom slippers
pair of slippers

smoke de|tec|tor /smoʊk dɪtɛktər/ (**smoke detectors**)

HOTEL ROOM: BEDROOM

NOUN A **smoke detector** is a device fixed to the ceiling of a room which makes a loud noise if there is smoke in the air, to warn people.

○ Safety precautions include smoke detectors in all rooms and kitchens.

○ *For safety, hotels must install fire doors and smoke detectors.*

▶ **SYNONYM:**
smoke alarm

---

smok|ing room /smˈoʊkɪŋ rum/ (smoking rooms)

HOTEL ROOM: BEDROOM

NOUN A **smoking room** is a guest room that can be booked by people who smoke.

○ *If you are in a smoking room and wish to smoke, get an ashtray from reception.*

○ *Please ask for either a smoking room or no smoking room.*

> **RELATED WORDS**
>
> The opposite of a **smoking room** is a **no-smoking room** or **non-smoking room**.

---

snacks /snæks/

HOTEL ROOM: BEDROOM

NOUN **Snacks** are simple foods that are quick and easy to prepare and eat.

○ *Complementary snacks are offered with drinks in the bar.*

○ *We serve light snacks at the bar all day.*

---

soap /soʊp/

HOTEL ROOM: BATHROOM

NOUN **Soap** is a substance that you use with water for washing yourself or sometimes for washing clothes.

○ *A bar of soap and two towels were left beside the bath.*

○ *Do the bathrooms have shampoo and soap?*

▶ **COLLOCATION:**
bar of soap

so|da wa|ter /soʊdə wɔtər/

HOTEL BAR

NOUN **Soda water** is carbonated water and is often used for mixing with alcoholic drinks and fruit juice.

○ *Add soda water to the fruit juice and stir.*

○ *He asked for a whiskey with soda water.*

soft-boiled egg /sɔft bɔɪld ɛg/ (**soft-boiled eggs**)

HOTEL ROOM: BEDROOM

NOUN A **soft-boiled egg** is one that has been boiled for only a few minutes, so that the yellow part is still liquid.

○ *She ordered a soft-boiled egg, toast with no butter, and tea.*

○ *Do you want hard or soft-boiled eggs?*

soft drinks /sɔft drɪŋks/

HOTEL ROOM: BEDROOM

NOUN A **soft drink** is a cold, nonalcoholic drink such as lemonade or fruit juice, or a carbonated drink.

○ *Can I get you some wine, or would you prefer a soft drink?*

○ *Many customers prefer soft drinks to alcoholic drinks.*

som|me|lier /sʌməlyeɪ/ (**sommeliers**)

HOTEL ROOM: BEDROOM

NOUN A **sommelier** is the person responsible for serving wine in a restaurant or hotel.

○ *The sommelier chose a bottle of wine for the customer.*

○ *If you like the wine, the sommelier will pour it into your glass.*

▶ SYNONYM:
wine waiter

soup bowl /sup boʊl/ (**soup bowls**)

HOTEL ROOM: BEDROOM

NOUN A **soup bowl** is a bowl, usually wider and more shallow than a cereal bowl, in which soup is served.

○ Divide the soup between four soup bowls.

○ Soup served in a soup bowl is eaten with the soup spoon.

▶ SYNONYM:
  soup dish

soup spoon /sup spun/ (**soup spoons**)

RESTAURANT: EQUIPMENT

NOUN A **soup spoon** is a spoon used for eating soup. The bowl-like part at the end of it is round.

○ If you're serving soup, provide soup spoons.

○ Provide some bread and a soup spoon for customers who order soup.

spa /spɑ/ (**spas**)

HOTEL FACILITIES

NOUN A **spa** is a kind of hotel, or a part of a hotel, where people go to exercise and have special treatments in order to improve their health.

○ There is an excellent spa with a large pool and sauna.

○ The hotel's luxurious spa and health club opens this month.

spa and well|ness fa|cil|i|ties /spɑ ənd wɛlnəs fəsɪlɪtiz/

HOTEL FACILITIES

NOUN In a hotel, the **spa and wellness facilities** are where people go to exercise and have special treatments in order to improve their health.

○ The spa and wellness facilities include a sauna and treatment rooms.

○ The spa and wellness facilities include a sauna and gym.

S

spare ribs /spɛər rɪbz/

HOTEL FACILITIES

NOUN **Spare ribs** are pieces of meat such as beef or pork that have been cut to include one of the animal's ribs.

○ *Chinese-style spare ribs are served with Sichuan sauce.*

○ *Lamb chops and spare ribs are on the menu.*

spar|kling min|er|al wa|ter /spɑrklɪŋ mɪnərəl wɔtər/ (**sparkling mineral waters**)

HOTEL BAR

COUNT/NONCOUNT NOUN **Sparkling mineral water** is mineral water that is slightly carbonated.

○ *They have no large bottles of sparkling mineral water, only still water.*

○ *I prefer still to sparkling mineral water.*

spar|kling wine /spɑrklɪŋ waɪn/ (**sparkling wines**)

HOTEL BAR

COUNT/NONCOUNT NOUN **Sparkling wine** is wine that is slightly carbonated.

○ *Sparkling wine is a good alternative to champagne.*

○ *The package offers accommodation for two and complimentary bottles of sparkling wine.*

▶ **COLLOCATIONS:**
 bottle of sparkling wine
 glass of sparkling wine

spir|its /spɪrɪts/

HOTEL FACILITIES

NOUN **Spirits** are strong alcoholic drinks such as whiskey and gin.

○ *We don't serve beer – only wine and spirits.*

○ *Spirits and other alcoholic drinks are available at the bar.*

S

spoon /spuːn/ (spoons)

RESTAURANT: EQUIPMENT

NOUN A **spoon** is an object used for eating, stirring, and serving food. One end of it is shaped like a shallow bowl and it has a long handle.

○ He stirred his coffee with a spoon.

○ Use a spoon to carefully pour the sauce over the meat.

> **RELATED WORDS**
>
> The following are types of spoon with a particular purpose:
>
> **dessert spoon**
> a spoon, which is midway between the size of a teaspoon and a tablespoon. You use it to eat desserts
>
> **soup spoon**
> a spoon used for eating soup. The bowl-like part at the end of it is round

steak /steɪk/ (steaks)

FOOD AND DRINK: MEAT

COUNT/NONCOUNT NOUN A **steak** is a large flat piece of beef without much fat on it. You cook it by grilling or frying it.

○ I'd like my beef steak very well done.

○ The steak is fried with onions and served with French fries and salad.

▶ COLLOCATIONS:
  beef steak
  salmon steak

store bag|gage /stɔr bægɪdʒ/ (stores baggage, stored baggage, storing baggage)

HOTEL FACILITIES

PHRASE If a hotel **stores baggage**, it puts a guest's baggage in a storage room until it is needed by the guest.

○ Can you store baggage in a storage room if the room is not ready?

○ You're welcome to store your baggage with us until you leave.

---

sug|ar¹ /ʃʊgər/ (sugars)

FOOD AND DRINK: BREAKFAST

NOUN If someone has one **sugar** in their tea or coffee, they have one small spoon of sugar or one sugar lump in it.

○ How many sugars do you take in your tea?

○ I like two sugars in tea and one in coffee.

---

sug|ar² /ʃʊgər/

FOOD AND DRINK: BREAKFAST

NOUN **Sugar** is a sweet substance that is used to make food and drinks sweet. It is usually in the form of small white or brown crystals.

○ She poured the tea and brought milk and sugar.

○ Do you want brown or white sugar with your coffee?

---

sug|ar cu|be /ʃʊgər kyub/ (sugar cubes)

HOTEL ROOM

NOUN **Sugar cubes** are small lumps of sugar shaped into cubes. You put them in cups of tea and coffee.

○ Place three sugar cubes in a coffee cup.

○ Stir the coffee until the sugar cubes dissolve.

▶ **SYNONYM:**
sugar lump

---

suite /swit/ (suites)

HOTEL ROOM

NOUN A **suite** is a set of rooms in a hotel or other building.

○ He chose the most expensive suite in the whole hotel.

○ Our two-room suites consist of a bedroom and a separate living room.

sun|ny side up /sʌni saɪd ʌp/

FOOD AND DRINK: BREAKFAST

PHRASE If a fried egg is served **sunny side up**, it is cooked on one side only, with the yellow part on top.

○ He wants his eggs sunny side up, rather than over easy.

○ To make an egg to be sunny side up, don't flip it over in the pan.

su|pe|ri|or room /supɪərɪər rum/ (**superior rooms**)

HOTEL ROOM

NOUN A **superior room** is a room in a hotel that is more comfortable or has better amenities than other rooms.

○ It is $245 for a standard room and $275 for a superior room.

○ Superior rooms have a beautiful view over the hills.

su|shi /suʃi/

FOOD AND DRINK: FISH AND SEAFOOD

NOUN Sushi is a Japanese dish of rice with sweetened vinegar, often served with raw fish.

○ What sort of fish can be used for sushi?

○ To make sushi, you must prepare the rice properly.

sweep /swip/ (**sweeps, swept, sweeping**)

HOUSEKEEPING AND MAINTENANCE

VERB If you **sweep** an area of floor or ground, you push dirt or garbage off it using a brush with a long handle.

○ They sweep the floor when the room is cleaned.

○ She swept the crumbs from the kitchen floor with a brush.

▶ **COLLOCATION:**
  sweep the floor

S

sweet|en|er /swiːtᵊnər/

FOOD AND DRINK: BREAKFAST

NOUN **Sweetener** is an artificial substance that can be used in drinks instead of sugar.

○ *There was no sugar, only sweetener.*

○ *I prefer coffee with cream and no sweetener.*

---

swim|ming pool /swɪmɪŋ puːl/ (**swimming pools**)

HOTEL FACILITIES

NOUN A **swimming pool** is a large hole in the ground that has been made and filled with water so that people can swim in it.

○ *The hotel has a heated indoor swimming pool.*

○ *Our swimming pool is available for fun or exercise.*

S

Tt

---

ta|ble /teɪbᵊl/ (tables)

RESTAURANT: EQUIPMENT

NOUN A **table** is a piece of furniture with a flat top that you put things on or sit at.

○ Half the restaurant tables were empty on Saturday night.

○ They have booked a table in the restaurant for nine people.

---

ta|ble|cloth /teɪbᵊlklɔθ/ (tablecloths)

RESTAURANT: EQUIPMENT

NOUN A **tablecloth** is a cloth used to cover a table.

○ I took everything off the table and changed the tablecloth.

○ There are white tablecloths covering the tables.

---

ta|ble|ware (in BRIT use **crockery**) /teɪbᵊlwɛər/

RESTAURANT: EQUIPMENT

NOUN **Tableware** consists of the objects used on the table at meals, for example, plates, glasses, or flatware.

○ Plates, bowls, and other tableware should match.

○ Serve food and drink in clean tableware.

> **WORD BUILDER**
> **-ware** = describing an object
>
> The suffix **-ware** is used in some nouns, showing what an object looks like or where an object is used: **flatware**, **silverware**, **tableware**.

t

tar|iff /tǽrɪf/ (tariffs)

RESERVATIONS AND CHECKING IN AND OUT

NOUN A **tariff** is a list of prices.

○ *Room tariffs are lower in hotels outside the city.*

○ *Prices are shown on the tariff board in the hotel reception.*

taste /teɪst/ (tastes, tasted, tasting)

FOOD AND DRINK: COOKING

VERB If you **taste** some food or drink, you eat or drink a small amount of it in order to try its flavor, for example, to see if you like it or not.

○ *Taste the food as you cook it and adjust the flavorings if necessary.*

○ *Invite the customer to taste the wine before you pour it.*

tea /tiː/ (teas)

HOTEL BAR

COUNT/NONCOUNT NOUN **Tea** is a drink made by adding boiling water to tea leaves or tea bags.

○ *He handed them each a cup of tea.*

○ *Would you like some tea or coffee?*

▶ COLLOCATIONS:
cup of tea
tea bag
tea leaves

tea|pot /tiːpɒt/ (teapots)

FOOD AND DRINK: BREAKFAST

NOUN A **teapot** is a container with a lid, a handle, and a spout, used for making and serving tea.

○ *She poured boiling water into the teapot.*

○ *How many spoonfuls of tea do you put in the teapot?*

tel|e|phone /tɛlɪfoʊn/ (**telephones**)

HOTEL ROOM: BEDROOM

NOUN The **telephone** is a piece of equipment that you use to talk directly to someone else in a different place. You use the telephone by dialing a number on it and speaking into it.

○ Hotels set their own charges for telephone calls from guests' rooms.

○ Hotels set their own charges for calls made from the telephones in the rooms.

▶ COLLOCATIONS:
answer the telephone
telephone call

tel|e|vi|sion /tɛlɪvɪʒᵊn/ (**televisions**)

HOTEL ROOM: BREAKFAST

NOUN A **television** or **television set** is a piece of electrical equipment consisting of a box with a glass screen on it on which you can watch programs with pictures and sounds.

○ There is a television in each room with a wide range of channels.

○ Turn on televisions in the rooms to make sure they work.

▶ COLLOCATION:
watch television

three-course meal /θri kɔrs mil/ (**three-course meals**)

HOTEL ROOM: BREAKFAST

NOUN A **three-course meal** is a meal that consists of three parts served one after the other.

○ A three-course meal in a local restaurant will not cost more than $10.

○ The three-course meal includes an appetizer, entrée, and dessert.

t

ti|dy /ˈtaɪdi/ (tidies, tidied, tidying)

HOUSEKEEPING AND MAINTENANCE

VERB When you **tidy** a place such as a room or closet, you make it neat by putting things in their proper places.

○ The cleaner will tidy your room every day.

○ Housekeeping clean the rooms and tidy public areas.

tip¹ /tɪp/

FOOD AND DRINK: DINING

NOUN If you give a **tip** to someone such as a waiter in a restaurant, you give them some money to thank them for their services.

○ They gave the waiter a tip.

○ In a restaurant, a tip of 15% for good service is expected.

▶ **COLLOCATIONS:**
give a tip
leave a tip

tip² /tɪp/ (tips, tipped, tipping)

FOOD AND DRINK: DINING

VERB If you **tip** someone such as a waiter in a restaurant, you give them some money in order to thank them for their services.

○ It is usual to tip waiters, porters, and drivers.

○ We usually tip 18–20% of the bill.

toast /toʊst/

FOOD AND DRINK: BREAKFAST

NOUN **Toast** is bread which has been cut into slices and made brown and crisp by cooking at a high temperature.

○ Would you like some more slices of toast with your breakfast?

○ Have some bread or toast to eat with your eggs.

▶ **COLLOCATION:**
slice of toast

T

to|ma|to /təmeɪtoʊ/ (**tomatoes**)

FOOD AND DRINK: VEGETABLES

NOUN A **tomato** is a soft, red fruit that you can eat raw in salads or cooked as a vegetable.

○ She cut up tomatoes for a salad.

○ The sandwich is served with lettuce and tomatoes.

tooth|brush /tuθbrʌʃ/ (**toothbrushes**)

HOTEL ROOM: BATHROOM

NOUN A **toothbrush** is a small brush that you use for cleaning your teeth.

○ Most hotels have toothbrushes and toothpaste at the front desk.

○ We supply toothbrushes and razors to guests who forget them.

tooth|paste /tuθpeɪst/

HOTEL ROOM: BATHROOM

NOUN **Toothpaste** is a thick substance which you put on your toothbrush and use to clean your teeth.

○ Most hotels provide complimentary toothpaste and toothbrushes.

○ There are toiletries such as shampoo and toothpaste on the bathroom shelf.

tow|el /taʊəl/ (**towels**)

HOTEL ROOM: BATHROOM

NOUN A **towel** is a piece of thick soft cloth that you use to dry yourself.

○ Freshly laundered towels are provided every day.

○ Ensure soap and clean towels are always available.

tray /treɪ/ (**trays**)

RESTAURANT: EQUIPMENT

NOUN A **tray** is a flat piece of wood, plastic, or metal, which usually has raised edges and which is used for carrying things, especially food and drinks.

○ *The waiter carried the glasses on a tray.*

○ *He went to the room with coffee, orange juice, and toast on a tray.*

---

turn-down ser|vice /tɜrn daʊn sɜrvɪs/

HOTEL ROOM: BATHROOM

NOUN In a hotel, a **turn-down service** is the preparation of a room for a guest to sleep in by slightly turning back the comforter on the bed, turning down the lights, and so on.

○ *Turn-down service is performed in the early evening.*

○ *The turn-down service will also pull the drapes and put out the light.*

RELATED WORDS

The following are other services commonly offered by hotels:

room service/in-suite dining
a service in which meals or drinks are provided for guests in their rooms

laundry service
a service that washes and irons clothes for guests

valet parking
a service in which guests' cars are parked by an attendant

---

twin bed /twɪn bɛd/ (twin beds)

HOTEL ROOM: BEDROOM

NOUN **Twin beds** are two single beds in one bedroom.

○ *For larger groups, there are rooms with both twin beds and bunk beds.*

○ *The hotel rooms have one double bed or twin beds.*

T

Uu

---

u|ni|form /yˈunɪfɔrm/ (uniforms)

NOUN A **uniform** is a special set of clothes which some people, for example staff in a hotel, wear to work.

○ *The hotel staff wear dark blue uniforms.*

○ *The waitstaff don't have to wear uniforms.*

---

up|grade /ˈʌpgreɪd/ (upgrades, upgraded, upgrading)

TRANSITIVE/INTRANSITIVE VERB If you **upgrade** or **are upgraded**, you change your hotel room to one that is more expensive.

○ *You can upgrade to a larger room with a bath and views of the sea.*

○ *The guest was upgraded from a standard room to a superior room.*

---

up|per floor /ˈʌpər flɔr/ (upper floors)

NOUN An **upper floor** in a hotel is on a level above the first floor.

○ *Most people prefer rooms on upper floors.*

○ *There is an elevator to the upper floors of the hotel.*

▶ **SYNONYM:**
high floor

u

Vv

va|can|cy /ˈveɪkənsi/ (vacancies)

RESERVATIONS AND CHECKING IN AND OUT

NOUN If there are **vacancies** at a building such as a hotel, some of the rooms are available to rent.

○ *The hotel has a number of vacancies if you are still looking for a room.*

○ *Hotels that are usually full had vacancies all summer.*

vac|u|um (in BRIT use **hoover**) /ˈvækyum/ (vacuums, vacuumed, vacuuming)

HOUSEKEEPING AND MAINTENANCE

TRANSITIVE/INTRANSITIVE VERB If you **vacuum** something, you clean it using a vacuum cleaner.

○ *The chambermaid vacuumed the carpets today.*

○ *It's important to vacuum all the carpets and rugs regularly.*

vac|u|um clean|er (in BRIT use **hoover**) /ˈvækyum ˈklinər/ (vacuum cleaners)

HOUSEKEEPING AND MAINTENANCE

NOUN A **vacuum cleaner** or a **vacuum** is an electric machine that sucks up dust and dirt from carpets.

○ *Clean the carpet with a vacuum cleaner to remove any dirt.*

○ *Use the vacuum cleaner to suck up crumbs from the carpet.*

V

val|et park|ing /vælɛɪ pɑrkɪŋ/

HOTEL FACILITIES

NOUN **Valet parking** is a service that operates at places such as hotels and restaurants, in which customers' cars are parked by an attendant.

○ The hotel offers a valet parking service where staff greet customers at the entrance and take the vehicle to a parking garage.

○ The hotel has a private garage with security and valet parking.

PRONUNCIATION

Note the silent "t" in the word "valet."

---

val|u|a|bles /vælyuəbªlz/

GENERAL

NOUN **Valuables** are things that you own that are worth a lot of money, especially small objects such as jewelry.

○ Leave your valuables in the hotel safe behind the reception desk.

○ The hotel does not accept responsibility for guests' valuables or cash.

---

vin|tage /vɪntɪdʒ/ (vintages)

FOOD AND DRINK: ALCOHOLIC DRINKS

NOUN The **vintage** of a good quality wine is the year and place that it was made before being stored to improve it. You can also use **vintage** to refer to the wine that was made in a certain year.

○ This wine is from one of the two best vintages of the decade.

○ The sommelier will recommend the best vintage of a wine.

---

voice mail /vɔɪs meɪl/

HOTEL ROOM: BEDROOM

NOUN **Voice mail** is a system of sending messages over the telephone. Calls are answered by a machine which connects you to the person

V

you want to leave a message for, and they can listen to their messages later.

○ *Voice mail dramatically reduces the need for telephone assistance at the hotel's main switchboard.*

○ *To activate the voice mail service, dial 3 and follow the instructions.*

---

vouch|er /vaʊtʃər/ (**vouchers**)

RESERVATIONS AND CHECKING IN AND OUT

NOUN A **voucher** is a ticket or piece of paper that can be used instead of money to pay for something.

○ *Present the voucher and four people can eat for the price of three.*

○ *You will receive your discount vouchers on arrival at the hotel.*

V

Ww

wait|er /weɪtər/ (waiters)

RESTAURANT: PERSONNEL

NOUN A **waiter** is a man who works in a restaurant, serving people food and drink.

○ The waiters cleared the empty tables and laid them for dinner.
○ The wine waiter poured us some wine.

RELATED WORDS

Note that a **waiter** is usually a man who works in a restaurant, serving food and drink and a **waitress** is always a woman. Some people prefer to use the terms **waitperson** or **server** as they are used for both a man and a woman.

---

wait in a line (in BRIT use queue) /weɪt ɪn ə laɪn/ (waits in line, waited in a line, waiting in a line)

RESERVATIONS AND CHECKING IN AND OUT

PHRASE When people **wait in a line**, they stand in a line waiting for something.

○ I waited in a line to check in.
○ Customers waited in a line for 15 minutes before they were seated.

waitperson /weɪtpɜrsən/ (waitpersons)

RESTAURANT: PERSONNEL

NOUN A **waitperson** is a person who works in a restaurant, serving people food and drink.

○ *Your waitperson will be with you in a moment to take your order.*

○ *A waitperson said she could seat us in the back of the restaurant.*

---

wait|ress /weɪtrɪs/ (waitresses)

RESTAURANT: PERSONNEL

NOUN A **waitress** is a woman who works in a restaurant, serving people food and drink.

○ *The waitress brought their order.*

○ *The waitress poured him some coffee.*

---

wake-up call /weɪk ʌp kɔl/ (wake-up calls)

HOTEL ROOM

NOUN A **wake-up call** is a telephone call that you can arrange at a hotel to make sure that you wake up at a particular time.

○ *I booked a wake-up call for 4:45 a.m.*

○ *Could I have a wake-up call at 6:30 tomorrow?*

▶ SYNONYM:
alarm call

---

walk-up rate /wɔk ʌp reɪt/ (walk-up rates)

RESERVATIONS AND CHECKING IN AND OUT

NOUN The **walk-up rate** at a hotel is the price charged to a customer who arrives without a reservation.

○ *Guests without reservations will be charged the current walk-up rate.*

○ *If you do not book in advance, the walk-up rate for the hotel is $95 for a double room.*

---

wall sock|et /wɔl sɒkɪt/ (wall sockets)

HOTEL ROOM

NOUN A **wall socket** is a place in a wall where you can connect electrical equipment to the electricity supply.

○ *There is no wall socket for a hairdryer in the room.*

○ *There's a wall socket for electrical devices near the table.*

---

ward|robe /wɔːdroʊb/ (**wardrobes**)

HOTEL ROOM: BEDROOM

NOUN A **wardrobe** is a tall closet or cabinet in which you can hang your clothes.

○ *As well as the double bed, the room contained a set of drawers and a large wardrobe.*

○ *The bedroom had a large wardrobe and shelves for your clothes.*

---

warm /wɔːrm/ (**warms, warmed, warming**)

FOOD AND DRINK: COOKING

VERB If you **warm** food, you make it hotter.

○ *He warmed the milk in a pan.*

○ *If the food is cold, warm it a little in the oven.*

---

waste|bas|ket /weɪstbæskɪt/ (**wastebaskets**)

HOTEL ROOM

NOUN A **wastebasket** is a container for garbage, especially paper, that is usually placed on the floor in the corner of a room or next to a desk.

○ *The wastebasket hasn't been emptied.*

○ *The wastebasket is full of trash.*

▶ **SYNONYM:**
waste bin

---

well done /wɛl dʌn/

FOOD AND DRINK: MEAT

ADJECTIVE If something that you have cooked, especially meat, is **well done**, it has been cooked thoroughly.

W

○ Could I have the steak very well done please?

○ Allow the lamb an extra 10–15 minutes to cook if the customer wants it well done.

---

white wine /waɪt waɪn/ (white wines)

HOTEL BAR

COUNT/NONCOUNT NOUN **White wine** is wine that is pale yellow in color.

○ Red and white wine will be served.

○ I picked two bottles of white wine and one bottle of red wine.

---

wine buck|et /waɪn bʌkɪt/ (wine buckets)

RESTAURANT: EQUIPMENT

NOUN A **wine bucket** is a container that holds ice cubes or cold water and ice. You can use it to put bottles of wine in and keep the wine cool.

○ Place the bottle of wine in the wine bucket to the right of the diner.

○ Place unfinished bottles of wine in a wine bucket with ice to keep them cool.

---

wine cool|er /waɪn kulər/ (wine coolers)

RESTAURANT: EQUIPMENT

NOUN A **wine cooler** is a container for keeping bottles of wine cool.

○ Wine coolers are essential to keep your bottle of wine cool.

○ A wine cooler chills your wine to the correct temperature.

---

wine glass /waɪn glæs/ (wine glasses)

RESTAURANT: EQUIPMENT

NOUN A **wine glass** is a glass, usually with a narrow stem, which you use for drinking wine.

○ He brought her wine in a wine glass.

○ Hold a wine glass by the stem.

wine list /waɪn lɪst/ (wine lists)

RESTAURANT

NOUN A **wine list** is a list of the wines that are available in a restaurant.

○ They ordered dinner and asked for the wine list.

○ For full details of the food menu and wine list, please telephone the restaurant manager.

wire|less In|ter|net /waɪərlɪs ɪntərnɛt/

HOTEL ROOM: BEDROOM

NOUN **Wireless Internet** is a system of connecting to the Internet that does not need wires or cables.

○ Many hotels provide free wireless Internet.

○ Facilities in the rooms include a laptop with wireless Internet access.

w

Practice
and
Solutions

1. Find the words or phrases that do not belong.

1 Courses of a meal ....
   a appetizer **b** entrée **c** dessert **d** digestif

2 Types of glass for drinking ....
   a meal **b** beer **c** shot **d** wine

3 Terms relating to how well cooked a piece of meat is ....
   a rare **b** well rare **c** medium rare **d** well done

4 Staff in a hotel ....
   a busser **b** bartender **c** cocktail shaker **d** duty manager

5 Ways of serving eggs ....
   a scrambled **b** mashed **c** hard-boiled **d** sunny side up

6 Types of wine ....
   a sommelier **b** dessert **c** rosé **d** sparkling

2. Match the two parts together.

1 busser

2 duty manager

3 host

4 receptionist

5 sommelier

6 porter

a a person whose job is to reserve rooms for people and answer their questions

b a person whose job is to carry luggage in a hotel

c a person responsible for serving wine in a restaurant or hotel.

d a person who has overall responsibility for the way the hotel operates

e someone whose job is to set or clear tables in a restaurant

f a person who is in charge at a particular time

PRACTICE PRACTICE PRACTICE PRACTICE PRACTICE PRACTICE PRACTICE

3. Put each sentence into the correct order.

1 and coffee for / orange juice / we drank / breakfast / freshly squeezed

....

....

2 and some French / rare steak / fries / I ordered / a medium

....

....

3 side up / likes / sunny / Andrew / his eggs

....

....

4 toast / I asked / and / eggs / for scrambled

....

....

5 appetizer I / my / chose / for / the mussels

....

....

6 a tip / was so / the waiter / rude I / didn't leave

....

....

4. Rearrange the letters to find words. Use the definitions to help you.

1 **koctical** ....
(an alcoholic drink which contains several ingredients)

2 **ourqil** ....
(a strong alcoholic drink such as whiskey, vodka, and gin)

3 **host** ....
(a small glass of a strong alcoholic drink)

4 **tipaerfi** ....
(an alcoholic drink that you have before a meal)

5 **meghanpac** ....
(an expensive French white wine with bubbles in)

6 **seterds iwen** ....
(a sweet wine, usually a white wine, that is served with the sweet part of a meal)

5. Complete the sentences by writing one phrase in each gap.

> an accessible room   a single room   the ballroom
> the baggage storage room   the fitness center
> a conference room

1 I asked to leave my suitcase in ....

2 Most big hotels have ....
for business meetings.

3 I went to ....
before breakfast and did half an hour on the stationary bicycle.

4 My wife is disabled so we needed ....

5 There were people dancing in ....

6 I'll be staying there on my own so I only need

....

6. For each question, choose the correct answer.

| hors d'oeuvres | à la carte | prix fixe |

1 A menu in a restaurant that offers you a choice of individually priced dishes for each course is described as ....

| prix fixe | digestif | dinner plate |

2 A menu with a specific set of meals to choose from with a set price is referred to as a ....

| entrée | dessert | appetizer |

3 In a formal meal, the main course, or sometimes the dish before the main course, is called the ....

| calamari | aperitif | hors d'oeuvres |

4 Small amounts of food served before the main course of a meal are referred to as ....

| valet service | room service | turn-down service |

5 A service in a hotel by which meals or drinks are provided for guests in their rooms is known as ....

| appetizer | dessert | digestif |

6 Something sweet, such as fruit, pastry, or ice cream, that you eat at the end of a meal, is known as ....

7. Which sentences are correct?

1 A casserole is a dish made of meat and vegetables
that have been cooked slowly in a liquid.   ....

2 Cold cuts are thin slices of cooked fish which are served cold.   ....

3 An escalope is a thin slice of meat or fish on a bone.   ....

4 Pâté is a soft mixture of meat, fish, or vegetables with
various flavorings that is eaten cold.   ....

5 Spare ribs are pieces of meat such as beef or pork that
have been cut to include one of the animal's ribs.   ....

6 A fillet is a strip of meat or fish that has no bones in it.   ....

PRACTICE PRACTICE PRACTICE PRACTICE PRACTICE

8. Choose the correct word to fill each gap.

> pillow   mattress   bedding

1   Sheets, blankets, and covers that are used on beds are collectively
    known as ....

> sheet   duvet   blanket

2   A large square or rectangular piece of thick cloth that you put on a bed
    to keep you warm is a ....

> pillow   sheet   comforter

3   A rectangular cushion that you rest your head on when you are in bed is
    a ....

> duvet   sheet   mattress

4   A large cover filled with feathers or similar material that you use like a
    blanket is a ....

> comforter   sheet   mattress

5   A large rectangular piece of cotton or other cloth that you sleep on or
    cover yourself with in a bed is a ....

> mattress   crib   pillowcase

6   The large, flat object which is put on a bed to make it comfortable to
    sleep on is the ....

9. Put each sentence into the correct order.

1 the maid / empty / the wastebasket / to / I asked

....

....

2 and / the floor / then / I swept / vacuumed it

....

....

3 polished them / the tables / I dusted / and / then

....

....

4 the / the chambermaid / changed / sheets / had already

....

....

5 our room when / servicing / housekeeping / we arrived / were still

....

....

6 out / we were / was / restocked while / the minibar

....

....

10. Complete the sentences by writing one word or phrase in each gap.

| general manager | waitperson | maitre d' |
| housekeeper | doorman | bus boy |

1 A .... is a person whose job is to clean and take care of hotel rooms.

2 A .... is a person, usually a uniformed employee, who stands at the front of a hotel and helps people who are going in or out.

3 The .... of a hotel is a person who has overall responsibility for its running.

4 A .... is someone whose job is to set or clear tables in a restaurant.

5 A .... is a person who works in a restaurant, serving people food and drink.

6 A .... is the head waiter in a restaurant.

11. Find the words or phrases that do not belong.

1 Vegetables ....
   a celery b cauliflower c calamari d cabbage

2 Shellfish ....
   a mussels b clams c oysters d salmon

3 Fruit ....
   a lime b melon c cherry d carrot

4 Typical breakfast foods ....
   a casserole b granola c cereal d croissant

5 Soft drinks ....
   a brandy b root beer c soda d mineral water

6 Seafood ....
   a salmon b calamari c lobster d coleslaw

12. Complete the sentences by writing one word or phrase in each gap.

corporate rate	tip	cover charge
deposit	voucher	receipt

1 We took with us a .... that entitled us to a half-price meal for two.

2 I looked at the .... for our meal and saw that we'd been charged for a bottle of wine that we didn't order.

3 You have to pay a .... of twenty percent when you make a reservation.

4 We paid the hotel's ...., which was a little cheaper, as we were staying there on business.

5 If the service is good in a restaurant, I'll give the waiter a fairly generous ....

6 At the bottom of the receipt for a meal in a restaurant you'll often see a .... of about ten percent.

13. Rearrange the letters to find words. Use the definitions to help you.

1 semaeniti ....
(things such as stores or sports facilities that are provided for people's convenience, enjoyment, or comfort)

2 ira ditcinionong ....
(a method of providing buildings and vehicles with cool dry air)

3 subnises encret ....
(a room in a hotel with facilities such as computers and a fax machine, that allows guests to work while they are staying at the hotel)

4 tionnucf moro ....
(a large room where formal dinners or parties can be held)

5 toehl lomi ....
(a large and very comfortable car that is hired to bring guests to and from a hotel)

6 zucaJiz ....
(a large circular bath with jets that make the water move around)

14. Match the two parts together.

1 We'd finished the meal so
I called the waiter over to

   a confirm the reservation.

2 Carlo was too ill to go away so,
sadly, I called the hotel to

   b charge it to my room.

3 I wanted to pay for the wine so
I asked the waiter to

   c ask for the check.

4 When I knew for certain that
those were the dates, I called
the hotel to

   d make a complaint.

5 I wasn't at all happy with the
way that my room had been
cleaned so I went down to
reception to

   e show us to our table.

6 The maitre d' came to greet
us and

   f cancel the reservation.

15. For each question, choose the correct answer.

| accept a card | agree a card | admit a card |

1 To agree that a credit card can be used to pay a bill is to

....

| express date | terminal date | expiration date |

2 The date, written on a credit card, when it stops being valid is the

....

| deny a card | refuse a card | refute a card |

3 To not allow someone's credit card to be used to pay a bill is to

....

| reverse a charge | swap a charge | exchange a charge |

4 To put the amount you have charged back into the credit card account
is to ....

| credit card guarantee | credit card terminal |
| credit card holder | |

5 A piece of equipment that you use to read the information on a credit
card and charge a cost to it is called a ....

| credit card guarantee | credit card promise |
| credit card pledge | |

6 The arrangement that allows the hotel to charge a cost to your credit
card if you do not arrive on the day you arranged is called

....

16. Match the two parts together.

1	sparkling	a	egg
2	poached	b	breakfast
3	freshly squeezed	c	steak
4	Danish	d	orange juice
5	English	e	wine
6	medium well	f	pastry

17. Put each sentence into the correct order.

1 form that / in the feedback / was in / we filled / our room

....

....

2 food / about the / of the / we complained / quality

....

....

3 caused / we apologize / inconvenience this / may have / for any

....

....

4 complaints from / number of / customers about / we've had a / the service

....

....

5 hairdryer / that my / the receptionist / wasn't working / I told

....

....

6 our service / our guests / to leave / feedback about / we encourage

....

....

18. Which sentences are correct?

1 If you carve a piece of cooked meat, you cut slices from it.   ....

2 When you boil food, you cook it in oil.   ....

3 When you fillet fish or meat, you remove the bones from it.   ....

4 When you barbecue food, you often add a highly flavored
sauce to it.   ....

5 If you chop food, you cut it into many pieces.   ....

6 When you fry food, you cook it in hot water.   ....

19. Find the words or phrases that do not belong.

1 Alcoholic drinks ....
a beer   **b** liquor   **c** spirits   **d** club soda

2 Items used for cleaning ....
a brochure   **b** vacuum cleaner   **c** duster   **d** cloth

3 Words related to television ....
a flat-screen   **b** docking station   **c** channel   **d** remote control

4 Examples of flatware ....
a soup spoon   **b** butter knife   **c** pitcher   **d** fork

5 Bathroom vocabulary ....
a tray   **b** hot tub   **c** towel   **d** shaving mirror

6 Types of room ....
a accessible   **b** no-smoking   **c** single   **d** à la carte

20. Complete the sentences by writing one word in each gap.

> pitcher   menu   chef
> cognac   napkin   sommelier

1 I spread a .... on my trousers to keep them clean while I was eating.

2 The waitress brought a .... of water to our table.

3 The .... recommended a bottle of Argentinian red wine.

4 There were several very tempting dishes on the ....

5 The waiter said he would ask the .... to cook the dish without onions.

6 After the meal, we all had a .... with our coffees.

Solutions

Exercise 1

1. d digestif
2. a meal
3. b well rare
4. c cocktail shaker
5. b mashed
6. a sommelier

Exercise 2

1. e someone whose job is to set or clear tables in a restaurant
2. f a person who is in charge at a particular time
3. d a person who has overall responsibility for the way the hotel operates
4. a a person whose job is to reserve rooms for people and answer their questions
5. c a person responsible for serving wine in a restaurant or hotel
6. b a person whose job is to carry luggage in a hotel

Exercise 3

1. we drank freshly squeezed orange juice and coffee for breakfast
2. I ordered a medium rare steak and some French fries
3. Andrew likes his eggs sunny side up
4. I asked for scrambled eggs and toast
5. for my appetizer I chose the mussels
6. the waiter was so rude I didn't leave a tip

Exercise 4

1. cocktail
2. liquor
3. shot
4. aperitif
5. champagne
6. dessert wine

Exercise 5

1. the baggage storage room
2. a conference room
3. the fitness center
4. an accessible room
5. the ballroom
6. a single room

Exercise 6

1. à la carte
2. prix fixe
3. entrée
4. hors d'oeuvres
5. room service
6. dessert

Exercise 7

1. A casserole is a dish made of meat and vegetables that have been cooked slowly in a liquid.
4. Pâté is a soft mixture of meat, fish, or vegetables with various flavorings that is eaten cold.
5. Spare ribs are pieces of meat such as beef or pork that have been cut to include one of the animal's ribs.
6. A fillet is a strip of meat or fish that has no bones in it.

Exercise 8

1 bedding
2 blanket
3 pillow
4 duvet
5 sheet
6 mattress

Exercise 9

1 I asked the maid to empty the wastebasket
2 I swept the floor and then vacuumed it
3 I dusted the tables and then polished them
4 the chambermaid had already changed the sheets
5 housekeeping were still servicing our room when we arrived
6 the minibar was restocked while we were out

Exercise 10

1 housekeeper
2 doorman
3 general manager
4 bus boy
5 waitperson
6 maitre d'

Exercise 11

1 c calamari
2 d salmon
3 d carrot
4 a casserole
5 a brandy
6 d coleslaw

Exercise 12

1 voucher
2 receipt
3 deposit
4 corporate rate
5 tip
6 cover charge

Exercise 13

1 amenities
2 air conditioning
3 business center
4 function room
5 hotel limo
6 Jacuzzi

Exercise 14

1 c ask for the check
2 f cancel the reservation
3 b charge it to my room
4 a confirm the reservation
5 d make a complaint
6 e show us to our table

Exercise 15

1 accept a card
2 expiration date
3 refuse a card
4 reverse a charge
5 credit card terminal
6 credit card guarantee

Exercise 16

1 e wine
2 a egg
3 d orange juice
4 f pastry
5 b breakfast
6 c steak

Exercise 17

1 we filled in the feedback form that was in our room
2 we complained about the quality of the food
3 we apologize for any inconvenience this may have caused
4 we've had a number of complaints from customers about the service
5 I told the receptionist that my hairdryer wasn't working
6 we encourage our guests to leave feedback about our service

Exercise 18

1 If you carve a piece of cooked meat, you cut slices from it.
3 When you fillet fish or meat, you remove the bones from it.
4 When you barbecue food, you often add a highly flavored sauce to it.
5 If you chop food, you cut it into many pieces.

Exercise 19

1 d club soda
2 a brochure
3 b docking station
4 c pitcher
5 a tray
6 d à la carte

Exercise 20

1 napkin
2 pitcher
3 sommelier
4 menu
5 chef
6 cognac

SOLUTIONS SOLUTIONS SOLUTIONS SOLUTIONS

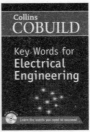

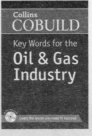